The Singer's Anthology of 20th Century Spanish Songs

Edited, with Introductions
and Translations
by
Josep Miquel Sobrer
and
Edmon Colomer

PELION PRESS
An Imprint of The Rosen Publishing Group, Inc.
New York

Published in 1987 by Pelion Press
29 East 21st Street, New York, NY 10010

First Edition
Copyright 1987 by Josep Miquel Sobrer & Edmon Colomer

Library of Congress Catagloging-in-Publication Data

The Singer's anthology of 20th century Spanish songs.

   Concert songs by Enrique Granados, Manuel de Falla,
and Frederic Mompou.
   Principally Spanish and Catalan words.
   Each song is accompanied by a word-for-word
translation and a syntactical translation into English
printed as text.
   Includes indexes.
   Bibliography: p.
   1. Songs, Spanish—20th century. 2. Songs, Catalan—
20th century. I. Sobrer, Josep Miguel. II. Colomer,
Edmon. III. Granados, Enrique, 1867–1916.
Songs. Selections. 1987. V. Mompou, Federico,
1893–. Songs. Selections. 1987. VI. Title:
Singer's anthology of twentieth century Spanish songs.
M1619.S599   1987   87-750986
ISBN 0-8239-0674-4

Manufactured in the United States of America

Contents

—*Introduction*

The purpose of this volume is to introduce concert songs by three outstanding Spanish composers of the twentieth century: Enrique Granados, Manuel de Falla, and Frederic Mompou. The volume is intended as a tool for singers and a companion to the music they will need for performance. The songs are grouped in cycles. Most of the cycles are the result of an organizing will of the composers, but for ease of usage we have gathered some independently published songs into groups. The groupings of songs with Spanish or Catalan titles are original; those with English titles have been grouped by the editors. Each song cycle is preceded by a note that explains culturally specific terms and gives a general idea of the circumstances of composition as well as of the general meaning of the poems.

Chapter One, "Pronunciation and Diction," discusses the idiosyncrasies of the sounds of Spanish and Catalan—the languages of most of the songs—and gives a detailed explanation of how to interpret the IPA symbols used throughout. Questions having to do with dialectological issues are also dealt with in this chapter.

Chapter Two, "The Composers and Their Times," introduces the composers with the intent of situating them within the general cultural and musical trends of the century. Chapter Three, "The Composers and the Poets," provides biographical and historical information about the authors of the lyrics. Both of these chapters can be read either as self-contained essays or as reference works; to that end they have been broken down into sections.

Chapters Four, Five, and Six form the body of the Anthology. With the exception of a few songs in French and one song in Galician, each song is presented as follows: The text of the song is accompanied by a phonetic transcription and a word-for-word translation; at the side of the page is the text of the song printed as a poem and accompanied by a syntactical translation into English. The system is designed to provide singers with as much basic information as can be given in printed form prior to their working with the melodic delivery of the songs. The transcriptions are given in the International Phonetic Alphabet (IPA), which is the system most likely to be familiar to nonlinguists.

The word-for-word translations are designed to inform the singers of the semantic context of each word they are to utter; they make little sense in English unless they are compared to the more syntactical translations. We may say that one version tries to make sense of words and the other of poems. The syntactical translations, however, lean more toward the literal than the poetic; the aim has been to produce a text that will help the understanding of the originals, not an artistic rendering to be read for its own sake.

The Anthology concludes with several appendices that will make cross references easy. Appendices A and B are historical summaries; Appendices C and D list the song titles and first lines with the song number and the page number where they appear. A general index closes the volume.

Throughout the Anthology we have aimed at presenting the texts of the songs as poems. Our idea was to help prospective singers feel the lyrical aspects of the song as would an educated native speaker when reading a poetic composition. Pronunciation may have to be adjusted slightly when working with the melody; our intention has been to set the appropriate mood of lyrical understanding previous to the musical delivery.

Practicality, then, is the guiding purpose of this volume; we hope that it will set the singers on a good course, even though we are aware that the written medium may go only so far when it comes to matters of diction and intonation. The book is designed to help singers and save them, perhaps, hours of coaching, but it cannot pretend to bring a novice to total control of the languages involved.

A work such as this is the fruit of collaboration. The Anthology is the responsibility of the two editors. Edmon Colomer has collected and organized the songs. He has made every effort to insure that the Anthology includes the complete works for voice by the three composers. Colomer is also the author of most of Chapter Two. Josep Miquel Sobrer has edited the songs and is the author of the phonetic transcriptions and translations. He has also written Chapters One and Three and prepared the Indices.

We wish to express our thanks to several people who have collaborated generously with the editors. The soprano Maria Lluïsa Muntada, who has performed many of these songs, gave us the wealth of her native command of the languages and of her professional experience. Two assistants, funded by a grant-in-aid from the Office of Research and Graduate Development of Indiana University, went beyond the call of duty to help Sobrer: Lisa Stouder helped make sense of the original drafts of many translations of difficult poems; Patricia Kathleen Minneman applied her keen critical eye to a wide range of materials—from the details of English style and punctuation to the general flow of the discourse in the introductory chapters. We are happy to recognize our indebtedness to them.

Acknowledgments

The following persons have granted permission to reproduce the copyrighted poetic texts in this Anthology:

Senyor Ventura Garcés for the poem by Tomàs Garcés.

Don Francisco Hernández-Pinzón Jiménez for the poems by Juan Ramón Jiménez.

Sa. Clara Janés for the poems by Josep Janés and her own.

Doña Claudia Periquet Rufilanchas for the lyrics by Fernando Periquet.

Senyor Jaume Portet Roma for the poem by Apel.les Mestres.

Chapter I

Pronunciation and Diction

The Hispanic world has a rich regional and national multiplicity. The works of the three composers studied in this volume naturally show that diversity. The texts presented are in two languages: in Spanish, and in Catalan, the language spoken in the northeast area of the Iberian peninsula. Catalonia represents the most vital of Spain's peripheral regions; it is an area with a broad cultural heritage, and its capital city, Barcelona, has been for some time a dynamic musical center. Two of the composers are Catalan; Granados and Mompou wrote both for Spanish and Catalan texts, Mompou wrote also for French and Galician.

Spanish has become a widely studied language in the English-speaking world. The orthographic rendition of Spanish is quite phonetic, especially when compared to that of English or French. But such relative accuracy should not deceive readers into the belief that they possess the ability to integrate text and music; nor can we deceive ourselves into believing that we are providing a foolproof guide. The lines of each song are transcribed phonetically using the International Phonetic Alphabet, but no phonetic alphabet can claim to reproduce perfectly the sounds of a language.

This chapter attempts to provide some guidelines and to propose some general considerations to help singers who are unfamiliar with Spanish or Catalan. It would be wasteful to present separate descriptions for each language, even though they have a distinct phonetic character. We have decided, instead, to present a complete description of their sounds, specifying those that are exclusively Catalan. A brief comparison of the two languages follows the phonetic explanations, and a list of suggestions for further reading closes the chapter.

Our transcriptions reflect the pronunciation of educated Madrid speakers for Spanish, and of educated Barcelona speakers for Catalan. We have not attempted to reproduce dialectal differences even though some pieces are clearly dialectal and regional in nature. Many of the songs, for example, are from the southern Spanish region of Andalusia and would ideally be pronounced in the dialect of that region. Several considerations, however, have discouraged us from attempting to transcribe those songs in the Andalusian dialect. The main reason is that a Spanish concert performer would normally render the songs, independent of their regional flair, in the educated idiom of central and northern Spain. Also there is no one Andalusian dialect—several subdialects may be diversely appropriate. Finally, since this book is designed for non-Spanish speakers, reproduction of such idiosyncratic details is not to be entrusted to even a careful phonetic transcription; rather it should be entrusted to the coaching of an expert. To compensate for the shortcoming we have just pointed out, we have included cultural notes on each cycle of songs and have enlarged our remarks on pronunciation and diction in this chapter with a brief explanation of the syntactical structure of colloquial Spanish.

Stress and Beat

Unlike other languages—most notably French—both Spanish and Catalan are not significantly different phonetically when spoken or sung. The one major difference between recited and sung poetry lies in the realm of stress. In a song, whether an art song or a popular tune, the stress pattern follows the beat of the music even though it may counter the usual stress in the spoken language. The word *corazón*, 'heart', for example, is always pronounced as an oxytone, with a clear stress on the last syllable: *co-ra-ZON*; in Falla's "Jota," however, it is sung *CO-ra-zon*. Native audiences will hear the correct *co-ra-ZON* in their mind's ear and at the same time will feel no violence to either speech or music. This is an instance of a prosodic syncopation that may appear quite frequently. The listener's ear is compensated by his or her knowledge of the language.

The phonetic transcriptions used include stress marks. They reflect the spoken rhythms rather than the beats prescribed by the composer. The singer, of course, will follow the rhythmic notation of the music when performing. But in our transcriptions we have chosen to reproduce as accurately as possible the sounds of the lyrics as they would be spoken by a careful, educated reader. The reasons for this decision are several. In the first place, since this volume is addressed to singers who will be performing in a language foreign to them, we felt it was important to provide them with an understanding of the poems both as units of meaning and as structures of sound. Second, we believe that in every song performance a creative tension must exist between the words and the music; the more so in the majority of cases presented here because the lyrics were written as poems previous to and independent of their role as song texts. Considering again the cultural background of our intended readers, we have endeavored to make them aware of the poems, an awareness that would come more naturally to native speakers. Third, we believe that language is essentially musical and that no song, whether artistic or popular, goes counter to the grain of the language. By stating these rhythmic dissidences we are providing our readers with the necessary awareness of the syncopation involved. The main stresses for each line are signified by a diacritical mark above the line ('); secondary stress is noted only when there may be hesitation, indicated by a diacritic below the line. Example:

no mostrose   ajeno
/no mos 'tɾo se a 'xe no
de que le amara
de ˌke le a 'ma ɾa/   (Granados, *Amor y odio*).

Other symbols

1. Conventional notation:

Italics are used for Spanish or Catalan orthography: *canción*, *cançó*.
Single quotes are used for English glosses: 'song'.
Parallel diagonal lines enclose phonetic representations:
/kan 'θjon/, /kən 'so/
Synalepha is marked by a crescent under the line as in the Granados example above.

2. Standard I.P.A. notation for vowel sounds:

a. Spanish vowels:

/i/ *hijo*, /ˈi xo/, 'son'
/e/ *que*, /ˈke/, 'what'
/a/ *mano*, /ˈma no/, 'hand'
/o/ *todo*, /ˈto ðo/, 'all'
/u/ *luto*, /ˈlu to/, 'mourning'

b. Additional vowels found in Catalan:

/ɛ/ *fred*, /ˈfrɛt/, 'cold'
/ɔ/ *mort*, /ˈmɔrt/, 'dead'
/ə/ *damunt*, /dəˈmun/, 'above'

3. Standard I.P.A. for semivowels:

/w/ *tuerto*, /ˈtwer to/, 'one-eyed'
/j/ *tieso*, /ˈtje so/, 'erect'
/ʝ/ *ya*, /ˈʝa/, 'already'

4. Standard I.P.A. for consonants:

a. Spanish consonants:

/p/ *pata*, /ˈpa ta/, 'leg'
/b/ *vara*, /ˈba ra/, 'rod'
/β/ *ave*, /ˈa βe/, 'bird'
/t/ *tapa*, /ˈta pa/, 'lid'
/d/ *dos*, /ˈdos/, 'two'
/ð/ *nada*, /ˈna ða/, 'nothing'
/k/ *casa*, /ˈka sa/, 'house'
/g/ *gato*, /ˈga to/, 'cat'
/ɣ/ *lago*, /ˈla ɣo/, 'lake'
/f/ *fama*, /ˈfa ma/, 'fame'
/θ/ *cera*, /ˈθe ra/, 'wax'
/s/ *paso*, /ˈpa so/, 'step'
/z/ *rasgo*, /ˈraz ɣo/, 'trait'
/x/ *mujer*, /mu ˈxer/, 'woman'
/tʃ/ *chico*, /ˈtʃi ko/, 'boy'
/ɾ/ *caro*, /ˈka ɾo/, 'expensive'
/r/ *carro*, /ˈka ro/, 'cart'

/l/ *palo*, /'pa lo/, 'stick'
/ʎ/ *calle*, /'ka ʎe/, 'street'
/m/ *cama*, /'ka ma/, 'bed'
/ɱ/ *confuso*, /koɱ 'fu so/, 'confused'
/n/ *mano*, /'ma no/, 'hand'
/ŋ/ *cinco*, /'θiŋ ko/, 'five'
/ɲ/ *año*, /'a ɲo/, 'year'

b. Additional consonants found in Catalan:

/ʒ/ *pagès*, /pə'ʒɛs/, 'peasant'
/ɫ/ *cel*, /seɫ/, 'sky'
/ʃ/ *caixa*, /'ka ʃə/, 'box'

Phonic Characteristics of Spanish and Catalan

1. Vowel Sounds

In phonetic terms a vowel may be described as a continuous voiced sound, in the formation of which air passes through the pharynx and mouth without audible obstruction. Two criteria are used to classify vowels: the height to which the tongue is raised in the mouth, and the part of the tongue raised highest.

Spanish has only five oral vowels, and Catalan eight, as opposed to more than twelve in English or French. Only when immediately followed by a nasal consonant does a vowel become less oral and resound in the nasal cavity; since this nasality is completely automatic, we have not marked it in the phonetic transcriptions.

The formation of vowels depends on the position of the tongue in the mouth cavity. Vowels articulated with the front of the tongue toward the palate are front, or palatal, vowels: /i/, /e/, *niño*, *nena*, 'boy', 'girl'. Those articulated with the back of the tongue raised toward the palate are back, or velar, vowels: /o/, /u/, *coma*, *muda*, 'I eat', 'mute'; /a/, *pata*, 'leg', is a central vowel.

In addition to these five vowels, Catalan has three more: /ɛ/, *pera*, 'pear', is the open *e*, somewhere between *e* and *a*; /ɔ/, *dona*, 'woman', is the open *o*, between *a* and *o*. In unstressed position both *a* and *e* are blurred into a medial sound, called *e* neutra in Catalan, /ə/.

The following chart should clarify the preceding explanation:

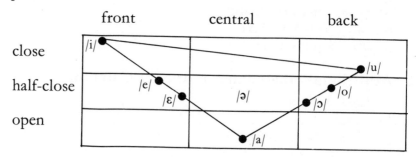

2. Description of Individual Vowels:

/i/ Close front vowel. Written *i*. The lips are spread, the front of the tongue is raised. Its timbre is similar to that of English *ee*, *ea* in 'tree', 'beak', but much shorter in duration.

/e/ Half-close front vowel. Written *e*. The lips are spread, the front of the tongue is raised. More close than the vowel sound in English 'pen', 'death', and distinguished, since it has no off-glide, from the diphthong of 'make', 'day', 'weigh'.

/ɛ/ Open, middle vowel. Written *e*. The tongue position is lower than for /e/; its sound is similar to the vowel in English 'death', 'many'.

/a/ Open central vowel. Written *a*. The most perceptible sound in Spanish. Lips are held wide apart, in a neutral position; the tongue lies low in the mouth. Spanish /a/ is considerably more open than English *a* in 'pat', and both shorter and more forward than *a* in 'far'.

/ɔ/ Open, back vowel. Written *o*. The back of the tongue is lower than for Spanish /o/. This is similar to English *o* in 'pot', 'mop'.

/o/ Half-close back vowel. Written *o*. Lips are slightly rounded, the back of the tongue is raised. Less open than English 'bog', 'saw'; it also differs from the vowel of 'home', 'noble' because its tongue position is much less advanced and contains no element of diphthongization.

/u/ Close back vowel. Written *u*; it is also the sound, in Catalan, of unstressed o. Pronounced with close lip-rounding and the back of the tongue raised high toward the palate. The timbre is similar to that of English *u* in 'rule' but the Spanish vowel is much shorter.

/ə/ Middle half-open vowel. Written *a, e*. This sound occurs only in Catalan and in unstressed positions. Whenever there is a shift of stress in a paradigm, /a/, /e/, and /ɛ/ automatically become /ə/. The sound is more definite, closer to /a/ than in the French 'mute e'; it is quite close to the English schwa.

3. Semivowels

Semivowels are gliding sounds that are not capable of forming a syllable. Semivowels may occur as on-glides, off-glides, or consonants, depending on their relationship with immediate vowels.

/w/ Labiovelar semivowel. Written *u, hu, ü*. In on-glides it is a voiced sound with close lip-rounding as for /u/: *prueba, bueno*, /'pɾwe βa/, /'bwe no/, 'proof', 'good'. In off-glides it is slightly tenser than the English *w* in 'cow' 'how': *jaula, neutro*, /'xaw la/, /'new tɾo/, 'cage', 'neuter'. Consonantal /w/ is the usual pronunciation of *hu* or *u* between vowels or as the initial sound in a syllable.

/j/, /ʝ/ Unrounded palatal semivowel. Written *i, y*, and in some dialects *ll*. In on-glides it is pronounced with voice and spread lips, the front of the tongue raised toward the palate. It is a more close and more pointed sound than English *y* in 'yellow'. The off-glide consists of a rapid transition between the vowel that precedes and the vowel /i/. Again, more close and more pointed than the nearest English equivalent: *y* in 'employ', 'annoy'. As a consonant, that is, between vowels or as the initial sound in a syllable, it is like the on-glide sound but pronounced with audible friction. This last sound is considerably sharper than its English equivalents; we transcribe it with the I.P.A. sign /ʝ/.

4. Consonantal Sounds

A consonantal sound is produced by the obstruction of the air channel. Three criteria are used to classify consonants:

  a. Action of the vocal cords. When vibration occurs, the consonants are voiced: when it does not, they are voiceless.

Contrasts between voiced, written first in the following list, and voiceless are: *b–p, d–t, g–k, ʒ–s*.

b. Manner of articulation. According to the way the air passes through the bucal and nasal cavities, consonants may be:

    stops: /p/, /b/, /t/, /d/, /k/, /g/
    fricatives: /β/, /ð/, /ɣ/, /f/, /θ/, /z/, /s/, /x/, /ʃ/, /ʒ/
    affricates: /tʃ/, /dʒ/, /ʝ/
    lateral: /l/, /ʎ/
    vibrant: /ɾ/, /r/
    nasal: /m/, /ɱ/, /n/, /ŋ/, /ɲ/

c. Point of articulation. According to the location of the obstruction of the air channel in the mouth, consonants may be:

    bilabial: /p/, /b/, /β/, /m/, /ɱ/
    labiodental: /f/
    interdental: /θ/, /ð/
    dental: /t/, /d/
    alveolar: /s/, /z/, /ɾ/, /r/, /l/, /n/
    palatal: /ʃ/, /tʃ/, /ʒ/, /dʒ/, /ʎ/, /ɲ/
    velar: /k/, /g/, /ɣ/, /x/, /ŋ/

5. Individual Consonants

We will extend our very summary descriptions only to warn of possible pitfalls for English speakers.

/p/ Voiceless, stop, bilabial. Pronounced with a sharp, crisp explosion of breath, it differs from its English equivalent in that the Spanish sound is not accompanied by the audible puff of breath or aspiration that characterizes the English stop. Lack of such aspiration is a mark of all Spanish stops, /t/ and /k/ particularly, in addition to /p/.

/b/ Voiced, stop, bilabial. Written *b, v*.

/β/ Voiced, fricative, bilabial. The fricative equivalent of /b/, it occurs whenever *b* or *v* is found between vowels, either alone or in the immediate company of *r* or *l*; a similar change in character, from stop to fricative, occurs in similar positions to /d/ and /g/. Failure to pronounce intervocalic *b, d,* and *g* as fricative is probably the most characteristic mark of an English or American accent in the pronunciation of Spanish or Catalan.

/t/ Voiceless, stop, dental. Written *t*.

/d/ Voiced, stop, dental. Written *d*.

/ð/ Voiced, fricative, interdental. Written *d*, the sound is automatically fricative except after a pause or following a nasal (the same environment affects *b* and *g* and makes them fricative /β/ and /ɣ/; *d*, however, remains a stop /d/ after /l/.

/k/ Voiceless, stop, velar. Written *c*, *qu*, *k*. There is no aspiration in this sound.

/g/ Voiced, stop, velar. Written *g*, *gu*.

/ɣ/ Voiced, fricative, velar. Written *g*, *gu*. Articulated with the back of the tongue raised toward the soft palate. Fricative /ɣ/ is the sound of *g* before *a, o, u* and of *gu* before *e, i*, in all positions except at the beginning of a rhythm group and after *n*.

/f/ Voiceless, fricative, labiodental. Written *f*.

/θ/ Voiceless, fricative, interdental. Written *c* before *e, i*, and *ẓ* elsewhere. Very close to *th* in English 'thin'. In many parts of the Spanish-speaking world, principally in Andalusia and Latin America, this sound does not occur and is replaced by /s/ in all positions. The sound /θ/ does not exist in Catalan either.

/z/ Voiced, fricative, alveolar. Written *s*; in Catalan *s* and *ẓ*. In Spanish it occurs automatically when *s* is followed by a voiced consonant: *rasgo*, /'raz ɣo/, 'trait'. In Catalan it is the normal pronunciation of intervocalic *s*: *rosa*, /'rɔ za/, 'rose', contrasting with Spanish /'ro sa/.

/s/ Voiceless, fricative, alveolar. Written *s, x*, and in Catalan *s, ss*, and *ç*. Castilian and Catalan /s/ differs from English mostly by its retroflex character: the tip of the tongue reaches upward, leaving a small, rounded opening between tongue and alveoles in the center of the mouth. In Latin America and Andalusia /s/ is pronounced very weakly or is aspirated, and it even disappears when syllable-final.

/x/ Voiceless, fricative, velar. Written *j* before *a, o, u* and before *e, i*, written *g*. It is a stronger sound than the final one in the Scottish word 'loch'. The back of the tongue is raised high against the soft palate constricting but not stopping the flow of air. This sound does not occur in Catalan.

/ʃ/ Voiceless, fricative, palatal. It occurs only in words borrowed by Spanish; in Catalan it is written *x* or, after vowel, *ix*. It is equivalent to the final sound in English 'posh'.

/tʃ/ Voiceless, affricate, palatal. Written *ch*; in Catalan it is written *x* or *tx*.

/ʒ/ Voiced, fricative, palatal. In Catalan written *j* or *g* (before *e*, *i*). It does not occur in Spanish. Same sound as the English *z* in 'azure'.

/dʒ/ Voiced, affricate, palatal. In Catalan written *tj, dj, dg, tg*. Same sound as the initial sound in English 'june', 'jewel'.

/ɾ/ Voiced, vibrant, alveolar (flapped). Written *r*. In the most common variety of English *r* the tip of the tongue comes close but does not touch the teeth ridge; in Spanish and Catalan it taps once against the ridge as the vocal cords vibrate. /ɾ/ is the sound of *r* except when it is initial in a word or is preceded by *l, n,* or *s*.

Examples: *comparo*, /kom 'pa ɾo/, *precio*, /'pɾe θjo/, *perdió*, /peɾ 'ðjo/.

/r/ Voiced, vibrant, alveolar (trilled or rolled). Written *rr, r*. It is formed by a rapid succession of taps made by the tongue against the teeth ridge. This is the sound of *rr* and of *r* in initial positions and after *l, n, s*. Examples: *la rosa*, /la 'ro sa/, *alrededor*, /al re ðe 'ðoɾ/, *honra* /'on ra/, *Israel*, /iz ra 'el/.

Both *r*'s are perhaps the most unnatural consonantal sounds for a native English speaker. Neither *r* is a sound with an exact English equivalent. Trilled *r* is somewhat easier to produce than the other *r* and for this reason singers should be careful not to use it instead of the flapped single *r* sound. Native speakers of Spanish are inconsistent in their utterance of *r* in some situations. There are both dialectal differences (with which we need not deal here) and, more significantly, differences derived from carefulness of diction. In very carefully enunciated speech (and therefore in concert singing) the rule given above for the pronunciation of /ɾ/ and /r/ should be altered according to the following guidelines:

a.—Both /ɾ/ and r occur intervocalically (whether within a word or a group of words) according to spelling and meaning. In between vowels /ɾ/ is written as a single *r* and /r/ is written as *rr*. Examples: *caro*, /'ka ɾo/, *carro*, /'ka ro/. (This is the only situation in which utterance of one or the other will make a difference for the meaning of the word; singers must be especially careful not to confuse these sounds.)

b.—Only /r/ occurs at the beginning of a word and after *l, n, s*. Examples given above.

c.–Only /ɾ/ occurs after consonants other than *l*, *n*, *s*: *brazo*, /'bɾa θo/, *ladrón*, /la 'ðɾon/ etc.

d.–Only /r/ occurs before consonant: *arma*, /'ar ma/, *arte*, /'ar te/, *arde*, /'ar ðe/, *árbol*, /'ar βol/, *perla*, /'per la/ etc.

e.–In word final position the pronunciation of /ɾ/ and /r/ is determined by the following sound: /ɾ/ will be pronounced when followed by a vowel, /r/ when followed by a consonant. Thus in song No. 1: *por estar en lo profundo*, /poɾ es 'taɾ en lo pɾo 'fun do/ but *este amor callado*, /'es te a 'mor ka' ʎa ðo/.

Our phonetic transcriptions follow the above guidelines and we recommend these distributions of /ɾ/ and /r/. Some native singers also trill their *r*'s in combinations such as those in c.–above; such a practice may be used with moderation— excessive trill will be felt by native speakers as pretentious. The trilled *r* is often overused by singers who do not speak Spanish. Singers therefore ought to be very careful not to trill their *r*'s when written singly in between vowels. To pronounce *cara* as /'ka ra/ is both wrong and comical; while *pero*, /'pe ɾo/ means 'however', *perro*, /'pe ro/ means 'dog'.

/l/ Voiced, lateral alveolar. Written *l*. In Spanish the sound of /l/ is always clear, i.e., comparable to the English *l* as it occurs before vowels, but it is not velar. In Catalan *l* behaves very much like in English: It is considerably more velar in syllable-final position.

/ɫ/ Voiced, lateral, velar. /ɫ/ is the sound of *l* when it is syllable or word final in Catalan; it never occurs in Spanish. The sound of /ɫ/ is like the sound of English *l* in equivalent final positions as in 'total', 'angel'; in Catalan *total*, /tu 'taɫ/, *àngel*, /'aɲ ʒɛɫ/.

/ʎ/ Voiced, lateral, palatal. Written *ll*. English has no /ʎ/ sound; the nearest sound occurs in the combination *li* in words such as 'million', 'familiar' but the palatal lateral of Spanish and Catalan is articulated as one sound with the tongue held low touching the lower teeth while the top of the tongue makes ample contact with the palate and air escapes on both sides of the tongue.

/m/ Voiced, nasal, bilabial. Written *m*, *n*. When in a rhythm group *p*, *b*, or *v* is preceded by *n*, this is pronounced /m/. When *n* and *m* are in contact in the group *nm* there is usually an assimilation to /m/ or /mm/.

/ɱ/ Voiced, affricate, nasal, bilabial. Written *n*. Before *f*, *n* is pronounced as an *m* preceded by a *p* sound; the *f* is in those cases pronounced affricate. Exs.: *confuso* /kom'fu so/; *sin fuerza* /sim 'fwer θa/, *enfermo* /em 'fer mo/;

/n/ Voiced, nasal, alveolar. Written *n, m*.

/ŋ/ Voiced, nasal, velar. Written *n*. It occurs whenever *n* precedes a velar consonant. It is the same sound as *ng* in English 'sing', 'rung'.

/ɲ/ Voiced, nasal, palatal. Written *ñ, n* in Spanish, *ny, n* in Catalan. The nearest English equivalent is *ni* in 'onion' but it differs from /ɲ/ in the same way /ʎ/ differs from *li* (see above).

Combination of Sounds

When we say that Spanish has phonetic spelling, we are speaking relatively. Readers are advised to follow the individual text transcriptions rather than attempting to memorize the above information in the form of rules. Those unfamiliar with Spanish phonetics should keep in mind that the vicinity of one sound often affects the quality of another. Writing is, in general, closer to etymology than it is to sound. The letter *m*, for example, is not always pronounced /m/, and the sound /m/ is not always written *m*. The letter *h* (except with the combination *ch* /tʃ/) is never pronounced in Spanish and only very occasionally in Catalan. It is a mere etymological fossil. Any behavior we have described for words beginning with a vowel is also true of words beginning with a vowel preceded by *h*.

1.   It may be worthwhile to bear in mind a few general caveats: Stops (/t/ and /k/ principally) are always unaspirated in both Spanish and Catalan; those whose native language is English will have to make the effort to pronounce them without the bursting flow of air that naturally follows them in that language. Stop or plosive sounds (alone or in combination with *l, r*) become fricative between vowels: /b/, /d/, /g/ become, respectively, /β/, /ð/, /ɣ/. This is true not only of groups within a word but also of groups within a rhythm unit. Consequently, a word like *donde*, 'where', is pronounced /'don de/ after a pause or a consonant, but it is pronounced /'ðon de/ if it follows, say, the preposition *a: a donde*.

Similarly /s/ becomes /z/ when it occurs immediately before a voiced consonant: *hombres,* 'men', /'om bɾes/, but *los hombres malos,* 'the bad men', /los 'om bɾez 'ma los/. Comparable transformations affect *m* and *n,* as noted above.

2. Syllabification. It is not entirely true that we speak in prose. Spontaneous speech tends to be uttered in groups of some seven or more syllables (the eight-syllable group is very frequent in Spanish), governed by more or less the same rules that the discipline of metrics studies in verse. Lines of poetry, unless they are very dissonant, consist of one or more of these natural groups of sounds that we have called "rhythm groups." Our transcriptions do not indicate these groups (but rather the smaller group, the syllable) because we are dealing with poems of rather short lines and because, in each case, the melodic line of the song must be obeyed.

A syllable consists of a group of sounds organized around a resounding nucleus: a vowel. As a general rule, each syllable corresponds to each of the notes in the melody. Our transcriptions separate the syllables of the words according to their natural organization around a vocalic nucleus. The syllables thus distributed correspond to the usual orthography as well as to the usual way of printing the lyrics in music sheets. For example, the opening of Falla's "Preludios" appears thus: "Ma-dre, to-das las no-ches jun-to a mis re-jas." We transcribe it accordingly: /'ma ðɾe 'to ðaz las 'no tʃes 'xun to̯ a miz 're xas/.

The singer must be careful, of course, not to close the syllables pronouncing the final consonant or consonant cluster until the musical duration of the note has ended: The duration of the note should be supported primarily by the vocalic nucleus of the syllable.

3. Diphthongs. When two vowels vie for the nucleus of one syllable, we normally have a diphthong, in which case the weaker of the two vowels functions almost as a consonant and is transcribed as a semivowel. As the weak vowels are unstressed *i* and *u,* their transcription in a diphthong is /j/, /w/. When a diphthong is formed by the combination of *i*

and *u*, in Spanish the first sound tends to be weaker than the second: /ju/ or /wi/. The opposite tends to be true in Catalan: /iw/ and /uj/. In any case our transcriptions indicate the appropriate pronunciation.

4. Hiatuses and synalepha. Any combination of one of the strong vowels (*a, e, o*) with another strong vowel or with stressed *i* or *u* constitutes a hiatus. Normal educated pronunciation equals two syllables; in popular speech hiatuses are often reduced to diphthongs. Whether a hiatus corresponds to one note in the melody or two must be our guideline here, rather than any general rule. The reduction of a hiatus to a diphthong is known as syneresis. Pronunciation of Spanish and Catalan in recital is quite formal, but as many of our songs are popular and regional in origin and character, syneresis may be expected. Our transcriptions indicate it with a crescent sign under the line, the same sign used for synalepha.

The combination of vowels within a rhythm unit occurs most often between words, when the word ends with a vowel and the following word begins with a vowel. These cases give rise to what the metricians of Spanish verse call synalepha. Synalepha is simply the blending in one syllable of two vowels in adjacent words; unlike syneresis, such blending is mandatory, unless of course the words are separated by punctuation signs or belong to different lines, or in extreme cases the scansion calls for the extra syllable. Most often synalepha occurs between two equal vowels, as in *prolija ausencia*, in which one pronounces a single vowel, *a*: /pro 'li xa (a)w 'sen θja/. Again, the corresponding melody note or notes give the clue. We transcribe synalepha both with the crescent under the line and, when appropriate, with parenthesis around one of the two equal vowels. The crescent for synalepha is often found in music sheets.

Spanish and Catalan

With the collapse of the Roman empire, the Islamic conquest, and the subsequent slow rebellion against Islamic rule, the Latin spoken in the Iberian peninsula became considerably changed and fragmented. Other changes occurred throughout the now broken Roman empire: The political and cultural upheaval of the early Middle Ages resulted, linguistically, in the evolution of the Romance languages.

Out of many dialects, the Iberian peninsula developed the three main Romance languages that, along with the older, non-Indoeuropean Basque, form the four present languages of Spain: Galician to the northwest, a sister language to Portuguese; Castilian in the center; and Catalan to the east, spoken in Catalonia, Valencia, and the Balearic Islands. Of these languages Castilian expanded the most, both in the Iberian peninsula, southward, and in the New World, after the Castilian imperial expansion of the sixteenth and seventeenth centuries. After 1714, with the new, French-style monarchy of the Bourbons, Castilian was imposed as the official language throughout Spain. Yet Catalan has lost none of its vitality, even though it has been barred from public life for long periods. English speakers usually refer to Castilian as Spanish, a nomenclature not totally accepted in the Hispanic world but the one we follow in this volume.

As this is not a work of either language history or linguistics, our notes here must be quite summary; we believe, however, that they are necessary, given its bilingual nature.

A linguistic comparison of Catalan and Spanish would be long and involved; indeed, it still may be impossible to formulate it perfectly given the present state of linguistic science. We shall limit ourselves to some general observations in an effort to provide a basis for a cultural understanding of the variety of lyric production that has affected the music of twentieth-century Spain.

The main differences between Spanish and Catalan are of two kinds: sociological and linguistic. Sociologically, Spanish is the hegemonic, official language spoken throughout Spain and most of Latin America. Catalan is spoken natively by some five million people, a majority of whom also know Spanish and have been exposed to it at school and in the media. The cultural liveliness of the Catalan areas, however, makes this minority language an important cultural medium and, from a musical viewpoint, an almost equal rival to Spanish.

Spanish and Catalan are similar, both deriving from Latin.

They differ marginally in syntax and considerably in morphology. In vocabulary Catalan is also distinct; it is much closer to the Provençal dialects of southern France and to some Italian dialects. The basic house vocabularies of Spanish and Catalan, though not the learned or technical vocabularies, show great disparity. The main distinction between the two languages, however, lies in phonology. As the preceding descriptions show, Spanish is unique in having an extremely clear and simple system of five vowels pronounced practically with the same timbre in any contextual situation; there is no qualitative difference, for example, between stressed and unstressed vowels. This is very different in Catalan. Spanish relies greatly on the clarity of its vocalic system and tends to soften its consonants, even to the point of silence; *s*'s are often aspirated, and intervocalic *d*'s often disappear. The clarity of the vowel, and therefore of the syllable, is essential in Spanish; as a consequence, a majority of the words in the language are paroxytones: *cinco niños hacen panes,* /'θiŋ ko 'ni ɲos 'a θen 'pa nes/, 'five children make loaves'.

Americans who study Catalan after learning Spanish must often unlearn some linguistic habits acquired very laboriously: final *l*'s are again velar, and the vowels vary according to their position in the rhythm unit. Catalan not only has two kinds of *e* and two kinds of *o*, but it changes the pronunciation of *a*, *e*, and *o* in nonstressed positions. The clarity of the vowel system, therefore, is less crucial for the signification of the language. Latin words, moreover, have mostly lost their last syllable in passing into Catalan, and thus Catalan abounds with oxytones and monosyllables: *cinc nens fan pans,* /'siŋ 'nɛns 'fan 'pans/, 'five children make loaves'. Syllable-final consonants are much more prominent in Catalan than in Spanish. These are surely the principal reasons for Catalan's reputation among Spanish speakers as a harsh language.

Another considerable phonological difference is that Catalan did not develop, as Spanish did from the end of the fifteenth century, the two characteristic sounds /x/ and /θ/; it continued its system of sibilants, maintaining principally two of the phonemes, /z/ and /ʒ/, that were lost in Spanish at the end of the Middle Ages.

Colloquial Spanish

Each group of songs is preceded by introductory commentaries that attempt to clarify the context that a person brought up in the culture of Spain would know automatically. To avoid repetition in the notes, we point out here some idiomatic aspects of popular Spanish.

The word *que* is both a relative pronoun (meaning 'that', 'which' or 'who') and a conjunction (meaning 'that'). As a conjunction it often has a lax use and merely signifies relationship of some sort: consequence or causality. Spanish popular verse uses *que* in a variety of ways, taking advantage of the flexible semantics of the word. (See for example the '*Canción amatoria*' No. 7 by Granados.) *Que* is also used at the beginning of a sentence to indicate that the utterance is not a beginning but a continuation, as if it were the answer to a previous statement or question that we must imagine. We have used a variety of English words, and sometimes blanks, in translating *que*. The word *que* at the beginning of a sentence or even a poem is a clear mark of the colloquial, almost spoken style of the composition.

Words of endearment in Spanish are based on the addition of a diminutive suffix or simply on the assumption that the loved one is a smaller being, a child. The word *niña* ('child') may be applied to women up to their thirties. Other words for the beloved refer to abstract qualities (rather than to the sweet edibles typical of English); thus words like *cariño* ('affection'), *vida* ('life'), *cielo* ('sky' or 'heaven'), and *gracia* ('grace') are direct references to a person and the equivalent of such English terms as 'honey', 'darling', or 'sweetheart'.

As these notes must be brief, we close the chapter with a bibliography for those readers who would like to learn more about these languages.

Suggestions for Further Reading, in English:

Bowen, J. D., and Stockwell, R. P. *Patterns of Spanish Pronunciation.* Chicago: University of Chicago Press, 1960.
Dalbor, J. B. *Spanish Pronunciation: Theory and Practice.* New York: Holt, Rinehart and Winston, 1969.

Elcock, W. D. *The Romance Languages*. London: Faber and Faber, 1960.
Entwistle, William J. *The Spanish Language*. London: Faber and Faber, 1936.
Gili, Joan. *Introductory Catalan Grammar*, 4th ed. Oxford: Dolphin, 1974.
Harris, J. W. *Spanish Phonology*. Cambridge: M.I.T. Press, Research Monograph No. 54, 1969.
Macpherson, I. R. *Spanish Phonology: Descriptive and Historical*. Manchester: University Press, and New York: Barnes and Noble, n.d. (late seventies).
Tomás, Tomás Navarro. *Studies in Spanish Phonology*, trans. R. D. Abraham. Miami: Miami Linguistic Series, No. 4, 1968.
Posner, R. *The Romance Languages: A Linguistic Introduction*. New York: Anchor Books, 1966.
Saporta, Sol, and Contreras, Helen. *A Phonological Grammar of Spanish*. Seattle: University of Washington Press, 1962.
Spaulding, Robert K. *How Spanish Grew*. Berkeley and Los Angeles: University of California Press, 1943.
Stockwell, R. P., and Bowen, J. D. *The Sounds of English and Spanish*. Chicago: University of Chicago Press, 1965.
Yates, Alan. *Catalan*, "Teach Yourself Books." London: Hodder and Stoughton, 1975.

Chapter II

The Composers and Their Times

The frontiers shaping the nations of the contemporary Western world were established during the hundred-year period culminating in World War I. This territorial consolidation coincided with the most crucial period in the history of the art of sound. The center of Europe, while asserting its eminently intellectual approach to all creative activities (concern for structure, form, etc.), strongly imposed its aesthetic premises on all Western culture. The central European approach saw the spread of the twelve-note system as an inevitable consequence. The prevalence of such a system was the result of an evolutionary process that had been uninterrupted in the countries of Germanic culture at least since the Renaissance; the process is similar but not parallel to that followed in Italy and France. The musical scene in Italy was monopolized by opera for the entire nineteenth century; despite the great influence that the genre had on the development of the musical and theoretical phenomenon throughout Europe, Italian music remained secondary to, if not totally apart from, the process inherent in the evolution of the mainline creative idiom. The traditional singularity of the artistic phenomenon in France became, with Berlioz, a direct reaction against the Germanic influence; but this influence remained as strong as it was inevitable. Depiction, sound impression, apparent digression, and even color became consolidated in an aesthetic tendency that had begun as a minor movement. The various nationalist schools, born in response to a concrete sociological and political reality, were gathered under this new aesthetic sensibility and were directly influenced by it.

Russia, with Glinka and the *Kutchka* or The Five, was the leader in a revitalizing attitude toward autochthonous cultural values; similar revivals had sprouted but had been aborted in some nations of contemporary Europe in the recent past. Such a situation might be expected in Spain. At the end of the nineteenth century, Spain was politically, and therefore also

19

culturally, debilitated. Practically destroyed by the Napoleonic invasion, it had entered a crisis head-on—the crisis of 1898, which culminated in the loss of its last colonial possessions: Cuba, Puerto Rico, and the Philippines. After 1898 the reality of the country was deeply depressed. Spain was, at the same time, highly picturesque. The painter Francisco de Goya expressed this culturally prostrated reality in his great art, but Goya is an isolated figure in the art scene of eighteenth- and nineteenth-century Spain. Compared to him, the general poverty of the artistic scene appears even more dramatic. Musically, the nineteenth century is the century of the *zarzuela*, almost the only musical genre that existed. It was a willingly anachronistic genre, locked within itself, yet the only source of revenue for professional Spanish composers.

When considering the composers Granados and, most particularly, Mompou, we must refer to the culture of Catalonia, which is politically and historically associated with the other cultures of the Iberian peninsula, but which maintains a clear distinction by its language, its modes of life, and, consequently, its art. Mompou is the foremost figure in the development of music in twentieth-century Catalonia; for this reason we must evaluate his work in a geographical, social, and cultural context: the Catalan context. Although Catalonia feels a direct influence from the general political movements in Spain, it expresses its most singular identity through its idiosyncratic cultural modes.

To better understand the contribution of the great Catalan composers, we must consider Spanish music in the context of the European creative world. From the standpoint of the general Spanish musical scene, Manuel de Falla is the most representative figure, and perhaps unique. Falla died in 1946, leaving no successor. He was not the seed for a generation; his school begins and ends in Falla himself. The aesthetic credos of his contemporaries—Joaquín Turina (1882–1969) and Conrado del Campo (1879–1953)—lack the strength to behave as a nexus within a generation of individual figures. The Spanish Civil War (1936–1939) may be the determinant cause: The most relevant figures—the composers Salvador Bacarisse, Rodolfo and Ernesto Halffter, and Robert Gerhardt and the musicologist Adolfo Salazar—were exiled when Franco came to power and were forced to carry on their work outside of their native country. The spirit of renovation that shaped the work of those who remained in Spain—Jesús Guridi, Oscar Esplà—found no way of surviving the ideological and reactionary wave that filled Franco's Spain. At that time, the crisis that had beset Spanish musical life appeared most decisive: There was an almost total retreat from public activity and a spiritual disorientation directly affecting musical creativity. At the same time Spanish musicians felt the absence of any constructive norm that would respond to living creative principles and tie them to the Spanish vital essence. The years immediately following the Spanish Civil War brought about the negation and the oblivion of the liberal and individualistic foundation necessary to a progressive European style. Spain, then isolated from Europe, remained in a passive state vis-à-vis the decisive turnabout that cultural and political European life suffered as a consequence of World War II. Spanish intellectual life came to be synonymous with reactionary aesthetic attitudes; the new official academic criteria, attempting to limit and mold artistic creation, produced a stifled art.

Around 1946 we detect the first symptoms of a cultural awakening in the northern parts of the Peninsula in favor of "freedom of expression." Barcelona, the capital of Catalonia, was at the head of the movement. In Barcelona, a small nucleus of musicians who favored a change of atmosphere created the "Cercle Manuel de Falla." This group represented an attitude that was paralleled in other artistic manifestations. The founding of the journal *Ariel* (1946) brought together such writers as Joan Perucho, Salvador Espriu, Jordi Sarsanedas, and Joan Triadú. The "Salons d'Octubre" (1948), followed by a nonconformist exhibition in 1963, lent a means of expression for the painters Antoni Tàpies, Tharrats, and Modest Cuixart and the poet Joan Brossa, all of whom published their manifestos in the review *Dau al set*.

Catalonia's distinctive life-style, expressed in all of its artistic forms, determined a kind of music that, because of its faithfulness to its country's personality, had no precedent in Spanish music. Between 1900 and 1920 a specific Catalan personality took shape as the consequence of a Catalan nationalist revival. The Catalans Isaac Albéniz and Enrique

Granados, working primarily before the twenties, tended toward an Iberian pannationalism; they are therefore not the best representatives of the Catalan musical personality even though their place of origin left a definite mark on their work.

Catalonia's geographic location has always facilitated contacts with Europe. Catalan culture, then, receives the vitalizing influence of foreign traditions. It was precisely at the turn of the century that the aesthetic tendencies responsible for the so-called Modern Style reached Catalonia and gave birth to a movement—*Modernisme*—to which several important figures belong: the poet Joan Maragall (1860–1911), the painters Isidre Nonell (1873–1911) and Ramon Casas (1866–1932), and the composer and musicologist Felip Pedrell (1841–1922). Later, symbolism and the Germanic nationalist affirmations brought about a transcendentalism that was assimilated, at least in intent, by a group of composers: Joan Manén (b. 1883), Jaume Pahissa (1880–1969), Enric Morera (1865–1942), and Pedrell himself. But the brief Catalan tradition in music was too weak to integrate such a spiritual burden.

The ensuing reaction to *Modernisme* was the more restrained *Noucentisme*. With this new movement, Catalan music began to find a more appropriate expression for its particular life-style, identified with the diaphanous light of the Mediterranean area, a feeling for orderliness, and the discovery of the lyricism inherent in the dynamism of everyday life. *Noucentisme* may well account for the fact that the ideal forms of Catalan musical creativity are short works. We are speaking now about a mature period in which we can point out an aesthetic mutation becoming apparent in the generation integrated by the composers Frederic Mompou, Manuel Blancafort (1897–1987), Robert Gerhardt (1896–1970), and Eduard Toldrà (1895–1962). The work of the first two, in particular, both demystifies the Wagnerian mood dominant in the early twentieth century and removes all solemnity from musical composition, thus taking it closer to more everyday activities.

Enrique Granados

The two main influences on Catalan music of the last quarter of the nineteenth century are Wagnerianism and nationalism, but it was mostly the latter that was exerted on the three main composers of the time. Of these, Felip Pedrell represents a genuinely Catalan attitude whereas Isaac Albéniz (1860–1909) and Enric or Enrique Granados manifest a dual nationalism, Catalan and Spanish. Pedrell's work as a composer is now mostly forgotten, but his influence on his younger contemporaries remains. Pedrell was the first Spanish composer to break successfully with the *bel canto* tradition by striving to create a lyrical drama based on Spanish folk song.

Enrique Granados y Campiña was born in the Catalan city of Lleida (Lérida) in 1867 and died at sea, near Dieppe, in 1916. He was returning from the New York (Metropolitan) premiere of his opera *Goyescas* when the steamship *Sussex*, in which he was crossing the English Channel, was torpedoed by a German submarine. The composer was last seen vainly trying to rescue his wife after they had both jumped overboard.

The young Granados had settled in Barcelona, where he studied piano with Francesc Jurnet and Joan Baptista Pujol (1835–1898). In 1883 he began studying composition with Felip Pedrell. Between 1887 and 1889 he lived in Paris, where he took private lessons from Charles Bériot and made the acquaintance of the Catalan pianist Ricard Viñes. Granados had postponed his trip to Paris because of ill health; when he finally made it to the French capital he was too old to enroll in the Conservatory and was thus obliged to take private classes. For that reason Granados's formation is more thoroughly Spanish, unlike that of Manuel de Falla and Joaquín Turina, both of whom came under strong French musical influence. In 1889 Granados returned to Barcelona and developed his career as a composer and pianist. In 1899 he founded the *Societat de Concerts Clàssics* (Society for Classical Concerts) and in 1901 the *Academia Granados*, where he taught his notable piano technique. Granados was a supreme example of the Catalan piano tradition, which is characterized overall by an emphasis on clarity, color, and a mastery of the pedals. During this period he became involved with the *modernista* group of writers and artists, although he often left this Catalanist circle to exploit the Spanish themes that were to give him an international reputation. From 1905 he collaborated with such artists as Pau Casals, Jacques Thibaut, Joaquim Malats, and Camille Saint-Saëns.

His masterpiece is perhaps the piano suite *Goyescas*, from

which he later composed his opera of the same title. The word *Goyescas* refers to the Spanish painter Francisco de Goya (1746–1828) and to Goya's fondness for the colorful popular types of eighteenth-century Madrid known as *majos* and described later in this book in the notes to the *Colección de tonadillas*. The *Goyescas* piano suite premiered in Barcelona in 1911, in Madrid in 1913, and in Paris in 1914, all with great success. The stage version was presented by the Metropolitan Opera House in New York on January 28, 1916. That performance was the first ever presented in Spanish in that auditorium and also the first Metropolitan production of an authentically Spanish work in any language. It had been arranged by the American pianist-composer Ernest Schelling, who had been a student of Granados. In spite of the Italian-German tradition at the Metropolitan, *Goyescas* was a great success. Perhaps as a result of it, Granados was invited at the last minute by President Woodrow Wilson to give a recital at the White House, causing Granados to cancel his booked transatlantic passage on a neutral Dutch ship.

Other than the opera *Goyescas*, Granados wrote for the theater the *zarzuela María del Carmen*, which premiered in Madrid in 1898, and four lyric works based on poems by Apel.les Mestres. His symphonic production comprises *Tres danzas españolas* (Three Spanish Dances, 1892), *La Divina Comedia* (The Divine Comedy, 1908), and several suites, and for piano and orchestra, *La nit del mort* (The Dead Man's Night) and *Elisenda* (1912).

Granados's favorite instrument as a composer was the piano, however, and it is his keyboard music that has given him his reputation. Among pieces for piano he wrote *Doce danzas españolas* (Twelve Spanish Dances), *Siete valses poéticos* (Seven Poetic Waltzes), *Seis escenas románticas* (Six Romantic Scenes), *Capricho español* (Spanish Capriccio), and *Allegro de concierto*.

Granados sought his musical inspiration from all of the regions of Spain. If for Albéniz the most fertile of these was Andalusia, for Granados it was the city of Madrid; not the contemporary Madrid of the turn of the century, but the mythical Madrid of the eighteenth century immortalized by the early paintings and sketches of Goya. Granados was by no means impervious to Andalusian music, but he was more restrained than his colleague in his *andalucismo*. The Madrid of the festive and gallant *majos* and *majas* was the main drive behind his compositions for voice and piano such as the *Colección de tonadillas* (Collection of Character Songs). Here his always urban popularism brings to life the world of the early nineteenth-century theater song, the *tonadilla*. This was originally a piece performed between the acts of a *zarzuela* by a singer who appeared on stage wearing the costume from the show. Granados's *tonadillas*, however, moved significantly away from their seventeenth- and eighteenth-century origins. These *tonadillas* premiered in Paris in 1916.

Granados is also the composer of chamber music; his best-known piece is the *Quintet for Piano* of 1895. Granados's musical activity coincided with the flowering of the *modernista* movement. His refined musical sensibility was put to the service of Romantic aesthetics with notable influence from Schumann and Liszt. Together with Albéniz (who wrote too little for voice to be included in this anthology), Granados was the creator of the modern Catalan piano school.

Manuel de Falla

Manuel de Falla, one of the greatest artistic personalities among twentieth-century nationalists, devoted his entire musical career to the upgrading of Spanish music, not only through his own creative work but also through his collaboration in the rediscovery of the most authentic values latent in the folklore of Spain and most particularly that of his native region, Andalusia.

Manuel Maria de Falla y Matheu (1876–1946) was born in Cadiz, a cosmopolitan oasis as a port city on the Atlantic Ocean. He was first exposed to music in the bosom of his family, although that exposure may be unimportant in his later development. His childhood pursuits, however, had a special significance; among them were a game in which Columbus founded a city, and the construction of a puppet theater. These two activities represent lasting ideas that eventually held an essential role in the creation of some of his most important works.

Falla lived in Madrid from 1896 to 1907. There he acquired academic musical training; he also composed *zarzuelas*—a situation that was, at least for the time being, unavoidable. During that period he met Spain's greatest folklorist, Felip Pedrell, whose influence on Falla's intellectual formation was decisive; from their first encounter the composer remained sincerely grateful to Pedrell for his guidance. While in Madrid he also became familiar with a book, Louis Lucas's *L'Acoustique nouvelle* (1854), which was an essential factor in the changed orientation of Falla's attitude as a composer. In 1907 he won two competitions, for piano and for composition, the latter with *La Vida Breve* (The Short Life, 1904–1905). That same year he traveled to Paris, where he met Dukas, Debussy, Fauré, Ravel, and the Spaniards Albéniz and Turina; from all of them he received both ideological influence and professional and artistic help and recognition. *La Vide Breve* was his letter of introduction. It did not premiere until 1913 in Nice; later it was performed in the Paris Opéra Comique and finally in the Teatro de la Zarzuela of Madrid, in November 1914. From this period came his *Trois Chansons* (Three Songs), based on poems by Théophile Gautier. From then on, the doors of concert halls around the world were open to him.

That very year, World War I made him return to Madrid. A fruitful period ensued, from which we have *El Amor Brujo* (Love, the Magician, 1914–1915), *Siete canciones populares españolas* (Seven Popular Spanish Songs, 1914–1915), and *Noches en los jardines de España* (Nights in the Gardens of Spain, 1911–1915). During the period 1914–1918 Sergei Diaghilev, director and impresario of the Ballets Russes, commissioned from Falla *El sombrero de tres picos* (The Three-Cornered Hat, 1918–1919). From a further commission, this time from Princess de Polignac, came one of his own masterpieces, *El retablo de Maese Pedro* (Master Peter's Puppet Show, 1919–1922). In 1920 he moved to Granada, where he remained until 1939, though never losing touch with the outside world. Performances of his works became more frequent; in some of them Falla himself participated either as soloist or conductor. This period was characterized by a special dynamism. Falla organized the first competition-festival of *cante jondo*, with the poet Federico García Lorca, in Granada; he also created the

Orquesta Bética de Cámara (Andalusian Chamber Orchestra), and composed his *Concerto for Keyboard and Five Instruments* (1923) and *Psyché* (1924). Falla was decorated with the Cross of the Legion of Honor and succeeded Edward Elgar in the Académie des Beaux Arts of France.

In 1939, in weakened health, Falla traveled to Argentina, where he conducted his last concerts. He died in Alta Gracia, in the province of Córdoba, Argentina, on November 14, 1946, leaving his stage cantata *L'Atlàntida* (Atlantis) unfinished.

The exoticism that came with the image of a festive Spain, *la España de la pandereta* or "Tambourine Spain," and which was represented by the "Spanish style" created in the eighteenth century with the *tonadillas* and street music, attracted many a composer, among them Bizet, Lalo, and Rimski-Korsakov; but their work, rather than examining the essence of the popular spirit, remained superficial. Debussy and Ravel presented a much more subtle approach, although their inspiration came to them indirectly as well. One may not speak of any authentic approach until the moment when Albéniz and Falla entered the European musical scene. Falla's contribution is based on his unfailing integrity vis-à-vis popular music. All his work, without exception, reflects a deep, honest understanding of his sources of inspiration. Pedrell's influence was a major factor in Falla's commitment to the study and research of Spanish music, both popular and learned. His art is a close parallel to that of Kodály and Bartók in Hungary.

In the work of Manuel de Falla, the influence of *cante jondo* is most significant. The purest form of flamenco, *cante jondo* is a song of depth, of the tragic sense of life; like the contemporary paintings of Picasso and Nonell, it awakens echoes from prisons and brothels. The human voice and the guitar are the media that this music employs in a singular fashion. The melodic gestures correspond to a text half sung and half recited; the peculiar guitar accompaniment adds a fundamental element to Falla's conception of the world of sound. His songs incorporate the rhythmic and melodic effects of the *Preludios* in the songs or dances with no other intention but that of working the audience's emotions. The harmonic effects, unconsciously achieved by the Andalusian guitarists, and the

tone color of the plucked instrument itself make for a
punctilious language, both austere and transparent, which
evades all massiveness. Guitar, as Falla would say, is not an
instrument for Romantic music. Yet Falla's natural craftsman-
ship became richer and perfected—first through Dukas's
advice, and later through his contacts with the French avant-
garde and with Debussy in particular. The influences of the
guitar tradition and of French avant-garde music were com-
plemented and assimilated through his continuing studies and
performance of the music of Domenico Scarlatti, the discovery
of which he owed to Pedrell. Falla recognized in the work of
this Renaissance master the value of the harmonic and tonal
effects of the guitar.

The *Siete canciones populares españolas* were meant to be
performed as a whole, although they do not constitute a cycle.
They were dedicated to Madame Ida Godebska and were
published by Max Eschig in Paris in 1922. The poems and
melodies were selected by Falla himself; all come from
traditional sources. Falla seldom used a melody in its popular
form, but although several of these songs are slightly modi-
fied, they all maintain their authentic air. The accompaniment
was written with the original forms in mind—a music with
which the composer felt completely familiar. The first two
songs, "El paño moruno" and "Seguidilla murciana," origi-
nate in the region of Murcia. "Asturiana," in the form of a
lament, comes from the north of Spain. The "Jota" is from
Aragón. Set between the fifth and seventh songs, "Canción" is
an evocation of resigned love and stands in sharp contrast to
the marked Oriental character of the song preceding it.
"Nana" is a lullaby; "Polo" is a perfect example of *cante jondo*,
with its characteristic melodic inflections, such as the shouting
of "Ay"; its piano accompaniment faithfully translates the
punctiliousness typical of the guitar.

The collection *Obras desconocidas* (Unknown Works, 1980)
brought together Falla's compositions for voice and piano that
were still unpublished. "Preludios," "Olas gigantes," and
"Dios mío, qué solos se quedan los muertos" were probably
composed between 1899 and 1901; they reflect the virtues that
characterized Falla's later works for voice: respect for the text

and a natural treatment of voice. "El pan de Ronda," written between 1914 and 1916, was to be part of a cycle that was never completed. The lyrics are by Martínez Sierra. Falla composed another song with lyrics by Martínez Sierra: "Oración de las madres que tienen a sus hijos en brazos" (1915), which preceded by one year Debussy's song with a similar theme, "Noël des enfants qui n'ont plus de maison."

Frederic Mompou

Mompou brought new interest and poetic depth to Catalonia's natural melodies and created an oeuvre essentially impregnated with the spirit of his land, with a tone at once intimist and transcendent. He was the first Catalan composer to create a balance between the expressive Catalan factor and its form, making the latter an ideal vehicle for nationalist expression. Although it would be hard to find precedents for his work, we may consider it to be of a triple spiritual parentage. In the conceptual order the influence of Chopin is most evident; equally important were the principles of harmonic freedom characteristic of French impressionism; and last we must consider the decisive influx of Scriabin's music. Elaborating on these influences, Mompou created his own aesthetic canon: an intuitive harmony, transparent and fluent, into which he poured his own feeling for dissonance, and which serves as a vehicle for communicating an unreachable, secret sense, almost inaudible. Mompou's ultimate intention was to lock up all communication within each particular work.

Frederic Mompou was born in Barcelona on April 16, 1893. As a young man he studied at the Barcelona Conservatory. For him the contact with Fauré's music was most influential. Mompou first heard a Fauré composition at a concert in Barcelona in 1909. Having determined to meet the famous French composer in person (a meeting that was never realized), Mompou traveled to Paris in 1911. His passion for music led him to abandon his career as a pianist. He then came into contact with a musical world that was to become fundamental for his own development as a composer. Mompou's work is capable of accepting and assimilating the most varied of spiritual influences. These influences do not show a distinctive mark from any particular school; however, the French sensibility had the most impact on his work.

In 1913 Mompou left Paris and returned to Barcelona, where he remained until 1921. From this period came his *Impressions íntimes* (1914), *L'Hora grisa* (The Gray Hour, 1916), *Escenes d'infants* (Children's Scenes), *Pessebres* (Nativity Scenes), *Cants màgics* (Magical Songs, 1917), *Fetes lointaines* (Distant Feasts), *Charmes* (1920), and his first *Cançons i Danses* (1918–1928). Once again in Paris, he remained there until the outbreak of World War I. His compositions from those years were limited to *Cançoneta incerta* (Uncertain Song), the first three *Comptines* (Ditties, 1926), and *Souvenirs de l'Exposition*. A second and definitive return to Catalonia in 1941 coincided with the consolidation of his creative principles. Although we may not consider Mompou a harmonic innovator, his refinement was a direct result of his own acoustic intuitions. His aim was to reach internal audition without contamination from the materiality of the sound-producing agent. For this reason, his communication is free, within the limits of possibility, from everything merely accessory; the essence of his thinking seeks to impose itself independent of aesthetic doctrines and modes that may have occurred during his long life.

After 1941 his works for voice and piano are *El combat del somni* (Dream Combat, 1948), *Cançó de la fira* (Song of the Fair, 1949), *Cantar del alma* (Song of the Soul, 1951), *Becquerianas* (1971), and *Cinc melodies* (1972) based on poems by Paul Valéry. His most significant collection for piano (three notebooks) is *Música callada* (Silent Music, 1957–1965). He has also written two ballets, *House of Birds* (1954) and *Perlimplinada* (1955); the cantata *Improperiae* for baritone, choir, and orchestra, and the children's cantata *L'ocell daurat* (The Golden Bird, 1970). Some of his compositions have been transcribed for orchestra.

The widening recognition of Mompou's creative personality has brought him many honors. He has been elected to the Acadèmia de Belles Arts de Sant Jordi (Barcelona, 1952); he was named Académico de Honor to the Academia de San Fernando (Madrid, 1973); and he received the Gold Medal for Artistic Merit (1976) from the Diputació de Barcelona, the 1977 Prize from the International Critics Club (Berlin), and a doctorate Honoris Causa from the University of Barcelona. He was honored by the Barcelona City Council and was awarded the 1979 Gold Medal from the Catalan government. It is gratifying to know that, now in his advanced age, Frederic Mompou is receiving much-deserved recognition at the three levels that his work spans—regional, national, and international.

Chapter III

The Composers and the Poets

T he composers represented in this volume derived their inspiration from a great variety of poetic materials. The poems they chose come from all periods, from the sixteenth to the twentieth century, and from all levels of rhetorical diction. They are the work of established classics and middle and minor talents, as well as of anonymous poets. The verses are in four languages: Spanish, Catalan, Galician, and French, a variety indicative of the relative novelty of the art-song genre among Spanish musicians. It would appear that in their attempts to introduce concert recitals to a Spanish audience the composers tried various kinds of poetic styles.

The three composers tapped the great source of poetry that is Spanish popular verse. Granados set to music many lyrics written by his friend Fernando Periquet, who also imitated or recreated the popular poetic style. In addition to popular songs, Falla used lyrics written by fairly minor poets, mostly his contemporaries and fellow Andalusians. Mompou shows the greatest diversity; it is difficult, if not impossible, to see a guiding line in his choice of lyric materials.

In this chapter we shall discuss the general poetic scene represented in this volume, considering the poets with a certain independence from the composers they inspired. The notes preceding the songs in the main section of the anthology throw light on the relationships between poems and music, between writers and composers. Here we shall try to provide a general overview so as to organize in the clearest possible way the information pertinent to the poetry presented.

Three songs by Granados, Falla's *Siete canciones populares*, and eleven songs by Mompou are based on anonymous popular pieces. An old tradition of popular lyric in Spain, dating back to the first occurrence of any text written in Hispanic romance, is the medieval *kharjat*. A *kharja* is a popular song that has been preserved in Arabic script (even though it was composed in an early form of Spanish) because of the fashion among learned Muslim poets to end their poems, called *muwashahat*, with a few lines from the popular lore. These contrastive Hispanic refrains of the *muwashahat* have thus preserved what otherwise would be a lost lyric tradition. In content the song tradition that starts with the *kharjat* tells of the emotions of young women, usually addressed to their mother, bewailing the departure or death of their lover. Much of the subsequent Spanish folk lyric has preserved the concise, sorrowful fictions of those very early poems.

Not all the anonymous lyrics truly belong to the authentic vein of popular poetry. Several songs are based on poems that have remained anonymous out of sheer oversight or editorial carelessness. Other lyrics have come down to us with their authors' names even though they are clearly attempts to recreate the traditional Spanish *copla* or popular song; the lyrics of Cristóbal de Castro and Martínez Sierra for Falla melodies are good examples.

Saint John of the Cross

Of the poets we know by name, the earliest is also the most distinguished: Joan de Yepes, better known by his religious name San Juan de la Cruz, or Saint John of the Cross. He was born in Fontiveros, near Avila, in 1542 and died in Ubeda in 1591. Saint John of the Cross was a Carmelite monk and a noted reformer of his order; his poetry is one of the peaks of Spanish literature and a classic of Western mysticism. His ascetic and mystical experiences inspired his short poetic production. Three of his poems, *Noche oscura* (Dark Night), *Cántico espiritual* (Spiritual Canticle), and *Llama de amor viva* (Living Flame of Love), prompted him to write four prose treatises as a doctrinal commentary. He also wrote a few brief poems, among which is the one put to music by Mompou: *Cantar del alma* (Song of the Soul).

Cantar del alma is a poem of stark simplicity. The metaphor of the fountain—the hidden water that comes to the surface to refresh and vivify—runs through the poem; the water here is an image for God, or divine love, or more concretely the Eucharist. The verses of the poem are variations on the water theme; they alternate with a refrain, unchanging: "Aunque es de noche" (Even though it is night). The night is a central image in Saint John's poetry; it symbolizes man's lot on earth, which on the negative side involves godlessness, and on the positive, the state of bewilderment preceding mystical ecstasy. Here, the alternation between the changing fountain imagery and the stable night metaphor creates the simple but forceful dynamism of the poem.

Antonio de Trueba

Of the four languages spoken in the Iberian peninsula, Basque is the only one not represented in this anthology. It is also the only Iberian language that does not derive from Latin, and its cultural and literary revival is more recent than that of the other languages. The only Basque poet represented here, Antonio de Trueba y de la Quintana, wrote in Spanish even though most of his themes have to do with his native region. He was born in 1819 and died in Bilbao in 1889. His most popular book was inspired by the Catalan poet Antoni Rubió i Lluc, one of the most important figures of the mid-nineteenth-century Catalan literary revival. Trueba's book *El libro de los cantares* (The Book of Songs) was published in 1851 and was responsible for the popular nickname given its author: "Anton el de los cantares" (Tony of the Songs).

Trueba represents a kind of poetry that flourished throughout nineteenth- and twentieth-century Spain and that derived its inspiration and its metrical forms from the popular lore. Other poets who followed this populist vein, among the authors represented here, are Apel.les Mestres, Cristóbal de Castro, Gregorio Martínez Sierra, and to some extent Josep Carner and Tomás Garcés. Besides his poetry and the journalism he practiced to earn his living, Trueba also wrote two one-act plays, short stories, and historical novels.

Gustavo Adolfo Bécquer

Both Falla and Mompou were inspired by the poetry of Bécquer; they both set to music one particular poem. Gustavo Adolfo Bécquer was born Gustavo Adolfo Domínguez Bastida in Seville in 1836. Like his brother, the painter Valeriano, he adopted the surname of an ancestor of Flemish origin, adapting the spelling to Spanish. He moved to Madrid, where he collaborated in several journals, wrote, and painted until his early death in 1870. Bécquer's poetic production consists of about one hundred poems published in several journals and as a book posthumously, under the unassuming title *Rimas* (Rhymes), in 1871.

Bécquer is a Romantic poet but he cultivated an intimist style, avoiding the rhetorical bombast of some nineteenth-century poetry. He also wrote short prose narratives, called *Leyendas* (Legends), in which he explored a poetic universe of magical landscapes and passionate feelings. Bécquer's poetry is today considered the high point of the Spanish lyric of the nineteenth century, rivaled only by the Galician poet Rosalía de Castro. Four main themes run through the *Rimas*: the definition of poetry or inspiration, the jubilant feeling of love, the gnawing pain of jealousy, and the melancholy provoked by the betrayal or death of the beloved. Bécquer's poetry has been praised and imitated by more recent poets because of its metaphorical daring; it is also the most popularly acclaimed of all modern poetry to the point that for Spaniards Bécquer has become the paragon of the poet.

Apel.les Mestres

Dated today around the more or less arbitrary date of 1833, Catalan literature had its modern revival. This movement, marked by regionalist enthusiasm, Romantic ardor, and a tinge of medieval nostalgia, soon came to be called *Renaixença* or Rebirth. Catalan literature, which had been dormant for two centuries, was reestablishing its place in the world and widening its readership among the people of the Catalan-speaking areas: Catalonia, Valencia, and the Balearics. One of the first celebrated Catalan poets of the new epoch was Joaquim Rubió i Ors, who collected his poems under the title and pseudonym of *Lo Gayter del Llobregat* (The Piper of the Llobregat River), but perhaps the most famous of all *Renaixença* poets was Jacint Verdaguer, the author of two impressive epic poems.

Later in the century the Catalan literary and artistic movement of the *Renaixença* was transformed into a more ambitious and internationalist movement known locally and throughout the Hispanic world as *modernisme* or *modernismo*. The modernist sensibility shares in the general European fin-de-siècle pessimism, with its typical *poètes maudits*, although, paradoxically, it represents a triumphant artistic moment with great emphasis on the interdependence of the arts—a paradigm of which was the figure of Richard Wagner. In Spain, Enrique Granados started his career within the main lines of the *modernista* movement, although he seems soon to have subordinated that decadent sensibility in favor of a sunnier, and commercially sounder, *españolismo*, a style celebrating the idealized world of the popular classes of eighteenth-century Madrid.

One of the now half forgotten poets of the *modernista* generation was Apel.les Mestres, who lived in Barcelona from 1854 to 1936. Mestres translated Heine into Catalan, and through Heine's influence he introduced into *Renaixença* poetry a style that was innovative in its evanescent and ironic romanticism. Mestres was an enthusiastic follower of the *modernista* style and became a prolific poet. Among the many poems of his long and productive life, his "popular" songs, many of which he himself put to music, are best remembered.

Mestres also translated Chinese poetry into Catalan through French and English mediations and wrote over sixty performed plays, most of them about fishermen of the Catalan coast. Mestres also wrote librettos for operettas. Three of these, *Petrarca*, *Picarol* (Rascal), and *Follet* (Little Fool), were set to music by the young Granados, who at that moment in his career was an active member of the Catalan *modernista* circle. Apel.les Mestres is also the author of short stories.

Countess of Castellar

Little is known about Isabel Maria del Carme Castellví i Gordon, countess of Carlet and of Castellar. She was born in Madrid on March 7, 1867, and died in Barcelona on May 21, 1949. Granados used her *Elegia eterna*, written in Catalan, but the only book she ever published was in Spanish: *Poema del cisne y la princesa, sonetos* (Poem of the Swan and the Princess, sonnets, Madrid, 1911). The title of that book and the verses of *Elegia eterna* denote a typical *modernista* sensibility.

Paul Valéry

The cultural attraction of France has been strongly felt in Spain both in medieval times and since the eighteenth century. The autonomist aspirations of the Catalans and the cultural narrow-mindedness of the Franco dictatorship, combined with the forced exile of many intellectuals after 1939, increased the ties with France during the middle of the present century. It is not surprising that Mompou would write for French texts such as those by Paul Valéry and the little-known Mathilde Pomès. Aside from this circumstance, Valéry has little to do with Spanish culture; we shall treat him here only summarily.

Ambroise Paul Toussaint Jules Valéry was born in Sète in the south of France in 1871. A well-known French symbolist poet and essayist, he published *Charmes* in 1922 and was elected to the Académie Française in 1927. He died in Paris in 1945 and was buried in the Sète 'seaside cemetery' that had inspired his most famous poem, *Le Cimetière marin*.

Fernando Periquet

The journalist, poet, and librettist Fernando Periquet Zuaznabar was born in Valencia in 1873; he moved to Madrid when he was sixteen and lived there most of his life. He died on August 25, 1940.

Periquet wrote art reviews and was a reporter for several newspapers. His interest in Spanish popular songs moved him to write a small book, *Apuntes para la historia de la tonadilla y de las tonadilleras de antaño* (Notes on the History of the Character Song and Its Singers of Old), which he had printed in Barcelona. As a poet he wrote the lyrics for the *tonadillas* put to music by Granados and included in this volume. He is also the author of the libretto for Granados's only opera, *Goyescas*.

Ramón Cabanillas

This anthology would not be complete without a representative of another of the established languages of Spain. Ramón Cabanillas came from the northwest region of Spain, Galicia, and wrote in its language, Galician, closely related to Portuguese. Cabanillas was born in Cambados (in the province of Pontevedra) in 1873 and died there in 1959. A member of the Spanish Royal Academy, he wrote in the traditional vein of popular forms with constant evocations of the Galician countryside. He also wrote for the theater. Cabanillas's complete works were published posthumously in Buenos Aires in 1959.

Cristóbal de Castro

The poet and journalist Cristóbal de Castro was born in Iznájar, in the province of Córdoba, in Andalusia in 1880. One of the founders of the *Academia de poesía española* (Spanish Academy of Poetry), Castro wrote novels, plays, and essays in addition to poetry. Among his books of poetry are *Cancionero galante* (Gallant Songbook) and *El amor que pasa* (Fleeting Love). In his poetic style he was a populist like so many of his contemporaries.

Juan Ramón Jiménez

One of the more universally known Spanish poets of the twentieth century, Juan Ramón Jiménez was born in Moguer, in the Andalusian province of Huelva, in 1881. In 1916 he married the woman who would be one of his main sources of inspiration, Zenobia Camprubí. At the outbreak of the Spanish Civil War (1936) he moved to the New World and settled in Puerto Rico, where he lived until his death in 1958. In 1956 he was awarded the Nobel Prize in literature.

His poetic production may be divided into two styles. The first style is very much in the line of *modernismo*, the main exponent of which was the Nicaraguan Rubén Darío. Juan Ramón Jiménez published *Arias tristes* (Sad Arias, 1903), *Jardines lejanos* (Distant Gardens, 1904), *Pastorales* (1905), and *Baladas de primavera* (Springtime Ballads, 1907). These poems are characterized by an air of musical nostalgia. Between 1908 and 1911 his poetry became more colorful and more forceful in rhythm and expression: *Elejías puras* (Pure Elegies, 1908), *La soledad sonora* (The Sonorous Solitude, 1908), and *Laberinto* (1911).

With *Diario de un poeta recién casado* (Diary of a Newlywed

Poet, 1916), JRJ (as he is often referred to) entered a new style, abandoning *modernista* sensibility in favor of a more intellectual set of themes and a painstakingly strict expression of feelings and ideas. The books that followed point to a constant elaboration in the new style: *Eternidades* (Eternities, 1917), *Piedra y cielo* (Stone and Sky, 1918), *Belleza* (Beauty, 1923), *La estación total* (The Total Season, 1946), and *Animal de Fondo* (Background Animal, 1949). JRJ is most popular in Spain for his book of short prose narratives about a little donkey in Moguer, *Platero y yo* (Platero and I, 1914).

Martínez Sierra

Another gentleman populist, Gregorio Martínez Sierra was born in Madrid in 1881. He wrote for the theater with great success and worked as a journalist and novelist as well. He also translated Maeterlinck and the Catalan Santiago Rusiñol into Spanish. As a poet and playwright he had the collaboration of his wife, María, who seems to be the actual author of the poem "El pan de Ronda" in the Falla section of our anthology. Gregorio's poetry has been described as possessing an elegant sentimentality and an almost feminine finesse—some credit for these qualities should surely be given to María. Martínez Sierra became well known with his book *El poema del trabajo* (The Poem of Work), published in 1898.

Josep Carner

Josep Carner i Puig-Oriol is one of the most important and influential poets of modern Catalan literature. Born in Barcelona in 1884, he soon began to write and publish: first for the stage, and later poetry. His first collection of poetry appeared in 1904, but it was not until the publication of *Els fruits saborosos* (The Savory Fruits) in 1906 that Carner found his definitive poetic voice. Thereafter he published more than a score of collections of poetry in addition to the journalism, theater, and translations with which he earned his living during his youth.

In 1920 Carner joined the diplomatic corps and left Spain; he was to live in foreign countries for the rest of his life. With the fall of the Spanish republic in 1939 Carner lost his consular position. He continued his exile, this time involutarily, as a professor first in Mexico and later in Brussels. He died in the Belgian capital in 1970.

Josep Carner's poetry always remained faithful to the ideas of the aesthetic movement in which he started, the *noucentisme*, a movement conceived in radical opposition to its preceding *modernisme*. The noun *noucentisme* or the adjective *noucentista*, meaning 'from the 1900's', was coined by the main ideologue of the movement, the philosopher and essayist Eugeni d'Ors.

For the *noucentistes*, poetry was above all an urban and civilizing activity, and the poem was ruled by strict and arbitrary laws of form. *Noucentisme* was essentially an antiromantic movement. An urbane and playful tone is central to all of Carner's poetry. His verses often describe, with tender irony and subtle idealization, archetypal figures—a middle-class bachelor, a seamstress—from the Catalan world. The visions of nature in Carner's verses are, as is typical of *noucentisme*, images of urbanized nature. He depicts groves rather than forests, and when he describes the sea it is calm and sunny and quietly traversed by the sails of fishing boats.

In 1957 Carner reorganized his complete poetic production to date, with many corrections and deletions. This new edition was reproduced in his *Obres completes* (Complete Works), published in 1968, and is now standard. It gathers many of his earlier books under one new title, *Lloc* (Place), as if this were a previously published work. The 'Uncertain Song' (*Cançoneta incerta*) that Mompou chose for his music is one of the poems from *Lloc*. The melancholy irony typical of Carner is evident in this piece, as is the vision of nature organized by some human element, in this case the pathway.

Manuel Blancafort

Another Catalan, Manuel Blancafort was born in La Garriga in the province of Barcelona in 1897. He is mostly a composer and only incidentally a poet. As a composer he became well known with the premiere in Paris of his opera *Parc d'atraccions* (Amusement Park). He has produced symphonic pieces as well as art songs and two string quartets. He died on January 9, 1987.

Tomàs Garcés

A younger follower of the *noucentisme*, the Catalan poet Tomàs Garcés i Miravet was born in Barcelona in 1901. His first book, *Vint Cançons* (Twenty Songs), from which Mompou chose his "Cançó de la fira," was published in 1922. Since then he has published six other collections as well as translations and criticism. Garcés can be considered among the populist poets like so many others in this anthology; but his popularism, showing influence of such poets as Juan Ramón Jiménez, Walter de la Mare, Jules Supervielle, and the Italians Montale and Ungaretti, is always delicately artistic and shows an uncomplicated but unfailing good taste.

Père Ribot

The churchman Père Ribot i Sunyer was born in Catalonia in 1908. Since 1941 he has lived in seclusion in the small town of Riells in the Montseny mountains. Between 1935 and 1975 he published nine volumes of poetry.

Josep Janés

Better known as a daring literary publisher, Josep Janés i Olivé was born in L'Hospitalet, near Barcelona, in 1913. As a poet he was influenced by Carles Riba and followed what could be called a *neo-noucentista* style. He published three books of his own poetry, the best known being *Combat del Somni* (Dream Combat, 1937). He died in an automobile accident in 1959.

Clara Janés

The youngest poet represented in our anthology is Clara Janés, the daughter of Josep Janés. Clara was born in Barcelona in 1940 but has lived in Madrid most of her adult life. Unlike her father, she writes not in Catalan but in Spanish. She has published seven books of poetry, translated Czechoslovakian poetry into Spanish, and written a biography of Mompou, *La vida callada de Federico Mompou* (The Silent Life of Frederic Mompou), for which she was awarded the essay prize by the city of Barcelona in 1972.

──Chapter IV

Songs of Granados

I. Colección de tonadillas

(Collection of Character Songs)
  I. "Amor y odio" (Love and Hate)
 II. "Callejeo" (Running the Streets)
III. "El majo discreto" (The Discreet *Majo*)
 IV. "El majo olvidado" (The Forgotten *Majo*)
  V. "El mirar de la maja" (The *Maja's* Gaze)
 VI. "El majo timido" (The Shy *Majo*)
VII. "El tra la la y el punteado" (The Tra-la-la and the Staccato)
VIII. "La maja de Goya" (Goya's *Maja*)
 IX. "La maja dolorosa" (The Sorrowful *Maja*)
  X. "Las currutacas modestas" (Fashion-conscious but Modest)

Nostalgia was surely the mood Granados wanted to convey when he wrote these twelve songs "in the old style." He used the lyrics of the now obscure Valencian poet Fernando Periquet (1873–1940), whose poems were popular among musicians of the early twentieth century; Albéniz, López Varela, and Bretón used Periquet's verses as well. He was also the librettist for Granados's only opera, *Goyescas*.

Three of the twelve songs are dedicated to María Barrientos, a famous lyric soprano who was born in Barcelona in 1884. Most of the songs in this collection are termed *tonadillas*, 'character songs', rather than *canciones*, 'songs'. A *tonadilla* takes its name from the verb *entonar*, 'to sing in tone, in key'. *Tonadilla* normally refers to a song performed in a theater. Granados wanted to produce a collection of songs with different emotions, from playfulness to mourning, but with an overall light character, such as one might hear in a theater or cabaret. Periquet's verses convey this popular style; the theme of the lyrics is the lighthearted and nostalgic evocation of some working-class neighborhoods in nineteenth-century Madrid.

These neighborhoods were the so-called *barrios bajos*, 'low districts' (the phrase nowadays means simply 'slums'), populated by people who have been idealized in literature and the arts (most notably by the painter Francisco de Goya) under the name *majos*. The word *majo* (and its feminine *maja*) was applied, at the end of the eighteenth century and the beginning of the nineteenth, to the artisans living in districts of Madrid such as Lavapiés and those surrounding the church of San Antonio de la Florida or the square of la Moncloa. The word *majo*, which would be the social opposite of *señor*, simply means 'pretty' except when it is applied, as in these songs, to characters from that time and those places. Spanish folklore has stereotyped an image of the *majos* as boisterous and happy-go-lucky people, arrogant in their speech, and typically wearing the showy costumes that were the inspiration for the bullfighters' "suit of lights." Since the word *majo* is culture-specific, we have left it untranslated here.

In order to understand the various allusions in these songs one must be aware of a few other aspects of popular Spanish culture. We shall summarize briefly the most pertinent.

Houses in the old Spanish style had only one or two floors. The outside windows on the first floor were protected by grillwork; flower pots were often hung from iron rings attached to the grill. Traditionally, courtship took place at such window grills, *rejas*, with the woman sitting inside and the man standing outside, as in "El majo tímido."

Goya painted two portraits of the Duchess of Alba. She posed nude for one and dressed as a *maja* for the other. The pictures are called "La maja desnuda" ('The naked *maja*') and "La maja vestida" ('The clothed *Maja*'); in both, the model is seen in the same reclining pose. Popular legend supposed Goya to have had an affair with his noble and married model, and to have used the "clothed" painting to divert the suspicions of the Duke of Alba. The song "La Maja de Goya," supposedly spoken by the Duchess, refers to that legendary love affair.

Smallness of foot is of course a sign of fashionable beauty, as expressed by the "modest" *currutacas* or fashion-conscious *majas* of the last song in this cycle. In Spanish popular speech, lack of basic modesty is humorously attributed to the death of the immodest person's grandmother: Since such a benign old lady can no longer praise us, as was her wont, we must be boastful for ourselves. The song alludes to the idiom "he or she has no grandmother" as an ironic euphemism for a braggart or an immodest person.

1
a 'moɾ i 'o ðjo
Amor y odio
Love and hate

pen 'se   ke   'ɟo sa 'βɾi a
Pensé   que yo sabría
I thought that I   would know

o kul 'tar la ' pe na 'mi a
ocultar   la   pena   mía
to hide   the sorrow mine

ˌke   poɾ   es 'taɾ en lo pɾo 'fun do
que   por   estar   en lo profundo
which because being   in the deep

nọ ‿ɑl kan 'θaɾa ‿(a) 'βeɾ el 'mun do
no alcanzaɾa   a   ver el   mundo:
not it would reach to see the world

ˌes tẹ a 'moɾ ka 'ʎa ðo
este amor   callado
this   love   silent

ke ‿um 'ma xo mɑl 'ba ðo
que un majo   malvado
that a *majo*   evil

Pensé que yo sabría
ocultar la pena mía
que por estar en lo profundo
no alcanzara a ver el mundo:
este amor callado
que un majo malvado
en mi alma encendió.

Y no fue así
porque él vislumbró
el pesar oculto en mí.
Pero fue en vano
que vislumbrara
pues el villano
no mostrose ajeno
de que le amara.

Y esta es la pena
que sufro ahora:
sentir mi alma
llena de amor
por quien me olvida,
sin que una luz
alentadora
surja en las sombras
de mi vida.

em mj ' al ma‿en θen 'djo
en mi alma encendió.
in my soul he lit

I thought I could hide my sorrow
since it was so deep that the world
would never see it —
This secret love that an evil *majo*
set ablaze in my soul.

i   ‚no 'fwe‿a 'si
Y no fue   así
and not it was this way

por k(e) ' el βis lum 'βɾo
porque   él vislumbró
because   he perceived

But it was not that way,
for he perceived the pain hidden
inside me.
But he perceived it in vain:
the villain did not dissuade me
from loving him.

el pe 'saɾ o 'kul to‿em 'mi
el pesar oculto   en mí.
the pain   hidden   in me

pe ɾo 'fwe em 'ba no
Pero fue   en vano
But it was in vain

So this is the sorrow I am now
suffering:
Feeling my soul ablaze with love
for one who neglects me and
leaves me
Without an encouraging light
to brighten the shadows of my life.

‚ke βis lum 'βɾa ɾa
que vislumbrara
that he perceived

'pwes el βi 'ʎa no
pues el villano
for   the villain

no mos 'tɾo se‿‿‿‿‿‿a 'xe no
no mostrose   ajeno
not did he show himself alien

de ‚ke le‿a 'ma ɾa
de que le amara.
that him I love

J   'es ta 'es la 'pe na
Y   ésta es la pena
And this   is   the pain

ke 'su fɾo a 'o ɾa
que sufro   ahora:
that I suffer now

sen 'tir mj 'al ma
sentir mi alma
to feel my soul

'ʎe na ðe a 'mor
llena   de amor
full   of love

por 'kjem   me ol 'βi ða
por quien   me olvida
for him whom me he forgets

ˌsin ke ˌu na 'luθ
sin que una luz
without a   light

a len ta 'ðo ɾa
alentadora
encouraging

'sur xa   en la(s) 'som bɾas
surja   en las sombras
coming out in the   shadows

de mi 'βi ða
de mi vida.
of my life

2
ka ʎe ˈxe o
Callejeo
Street watching

dos ˈo ɾas ˈa   ke ˌka ʎe ˈxe o
Dos horas ha   que callejeo
Two hours it's now that I walk the streets

ˌpe ɾo no ˈβe o
pero no veo
but   not I see

ner ˈβjo sa ˈʝa sin   ˈkal ma
nerviosa ya, sin   calma,
nervous   now without calm

ˌal ke   le ˈði koɱ ˈfja ða
al que   le di   confiada
he whom I gave in trust

el ˈal ma
el alma.
the soul

no ˌβi ˈom βre xa ˈmas
No vi   hombre jamás
Not I saw a man   ever

ke min ˈtje ɾa ˈmas k(e) el ˈma xo
que mintiera   más que el majo
who would lie   more than the *majo*

Dos horas ha que callejeo
pero no veo,
nerviosa ya, sin calma,
al que le di confiada
el alma.

No vi hombre jamás
que mintiera más que el majo
que hoy me engaña;
mas no le ha de valer
pues siempre fui mujer de maña
y, si es menester,
correré sin parar,
tras él, entera España.

———————————•———————————

I have been running for two hours,
nervous and disturbed,
but I cannot see
the man who took my soul in trust.

I never knew a man
more full of lies than the *majo*
who deceives me now;
but he won't escape from me
for I've always been a clever woman
and, if I have to,
I'll run after him
through all of Spain.

ke ˈoj m(e) en ˈga ɲa
que hoy me engaña;
who today me he deceives

mas ˈno le ˈa ðe βa ˈler
mas no le ha de valer
but not to him it will be of service

ˈpwes ˈsjem pre ˈfwi mu ˈxer ðe ˈma ɲa
pues siempre fui mujer de maña
for always I was a woman of smartness

i si ˈes me nes ˈter
y si es menester,
and if it is necessary

ko re ˈre sim pa ˈɾar
correré sin parar,
I will run without stop

tɾas ˈel en ˈte ɾa es ˈpa ɲa
tras él, entera España.
after him the whole Spain

3
el ˈma xo ðis kɾe to
El majo discreto
The *majo* discreet

ˈdi θen ke mi ˈma xo es ˈfeo
Dicen que mi majo es feo.
They say that my *majo* is ugly

Dicen que mi majo es feo.
Es posible que sí que lo sea,
que amor es deseo
que ciega y marea.
Ha tiempo que sé
que quien ama no ve.

'es po 'si βle ke 'si ˌke lo 'se a
Es posible que sí que lo sea,
It is possible that yes that so he is

ke a 'moɾ ez de 'se o ke 'θje ɣa j
que amor es deseo que ciega y
because love is desire that blinds and

ma 'ɾe a
marea.
dizzies

'a 'tjeŋ po ke 'se ke 'kjen
Ha tiempo que sé que quien
It's been time that I know that he who

'a ma no 'βe ·
ama no ve.
loves not sees

ˌmas si no 'es mi 'ma xo un 'om bɾe
Mas si no es mi majo un hombre
But if not he is my *majo* a man

ke por 'lin do ðes 'kwe ʎe j a 'som bɾe
que por lindo descuelle y asombre,
who for pretty he excels and astonishes

en 'kam bjo és dis 'kɾe to j 'ɣwar ða
en cambio es discreto y guarda
in stead he is discreet and keeps

un se 'kɾe to
un secreto
a secret

Mas si no es mi majo un hombre
que por lindo descuelle y asombre,
en cambio es discreto
y guarda un secreto
que yo posé en él
sabiendo que es fiel.

¿Cuál es el secreto
que el majo guardó?
Sería indiscreto
contarlo yo.
No poco trabajo costara saber
secretos de un majo con una
mujer.
Nació en Lavapiés. ¡Eh, ¡eh! ¡Es
un majo, un majo es!

———————————— • ————————————

People say that my *majo* is ugly.
And he may well be,
but love is a desire
that makes one blind and dizzy.
I have known for some time
that one in love cannot see.

My *majo* does not eclipse
or astonish anyone with his beauty,
but he is discreet, and he knows
how to keep
the secret I entrusted to him
because I know that he is faithful.

What is the secret that my *majo*
kept?
It would be indiscreet of me to
tell.
It would take some doing to
uncover
the secrets between a *majo* and a
woman.

He was born in Lavapiés.
Hey, hey! He is a *majo*, yes he is!

ke   'ʝo po 'se (e)n 'el   sa 'βjen do
que yo posé en   él   sabiendo
that I   placed in   him knowing

k(e) es   'fjel
que eś   fiel.
that he is faithful

'kwɑl 'es el   se 'kɾe to k(e) el   'ma xo
¿Cuál es el   secreto   que el   majo
Which is the secret   that the *majo*

ɣwar 'ðo
guardó?
kept?

se 'ɾi a____in dis 'kɾe to kon 'tar lo 'ʝo
Sería____indiscreto   contarlo   yo.
It would be indiscreet   to tell it   myself

ˌno   'po ko tɾa 'βa xo kos 'ta ɾa   sa 'βer
No poco trabajo   costara   saber
Not little work   it would cost to know

se 'kɾe toz de um 'ma xo kon ˌu na mu 'xer
secretos de un majo con una   mujer.
secrets   of a *majo* with a   woman

na 'θjo____en la βa 'pjes 'e   'e   'es
Nació____en Lavapiés. ¡Eh! ¡Eh! ¡Es
He was born in Lavapies Eh! Eh! He is

um 'ma xo um 'ma xo 'es
un majo, un majo es!
a *majo*   a   *majo*   he is

4
el 'ma xo (o)l ßi 'ða ðo
El majo olvidado
The *majo* forgotten

'kwan do re 'kwer ðes   los 'di as
Cuando   recuerdes   los días
When   you remember the days
pa 'sa ðos
pasados
past

'pjen sa em   'mi em   'mi
piensa en   mí, en   mí.
think   about me about me

'kwan do ðe 'flo res se   'ʎe ne tu
Cuando   de flores   se   llene tu
When   of flowers itself fill up your
're xa
reja
window-grill

'pjen sa em   'mi 'pjen sa em   'mi
piensa en   mí, piensa en   mí.
think   about me think   about me

'a
¡Ah!
Ah!

'kwan do en las 'no tʃ es se 're nas
Cuando   en las noches   serenas
When   on the nights   serene

Cuando recuerdes los días pasados
piensa en mí, en mí.
Cuandos de flores se llene tu reja
piensa en mí, piensa en mí.
¡Ah!

Cuando en las noches serenas
cante el ruiseñor
piensa en el majos olvidado
que muere de amor.

Pobre del majo olvidado, ¡qué duro
sufrir! ¡sufrir! ¡sufrir!
Pues que la ingrata le deje no quiere,
no quiere vivir, no quiere vivir.
¡Ah!

———————— • ————————

When you remember the days now past
think about me, about me.
When your window is full of flowers
think about me, think about me.
Ah!

When you hear the nightingale sing,
in the still of the night
think about your forgotten *majo*
dying of love.

'kan t(e) el ,rwi se 'ɲor
cante   el ruiseñor
sing   the nightingale

'pjen sa en   el 'ma xo (o)l βi 'ða ðo
piensa en   el majo olvidado
think   about the *majo*   forgotten

ke 'mwe ɾe ðe a 'mor
que muere de amor.
who dies   of love

'po βre ðel   'ma xo (o)l βi 'ðaðo 'ke
Pobre del   majo olvidado,   ¡qué
Poor   (of)the *majo*   forgotten   how
'ðu ɾo
duro
hard

su 'fɾir su 'fɾir su 'fɾir
sufrir! sufrir! sufrir!
suffer   suffer suffer

'pwes ke   la in 'gɾa ta le 'ðe xe
pues que la ingrata   le deje
since   the ungrateful him she leaves
no 'kje ɾe
no quiere
not he wants

no 'kje ɾe   βi 'βiɾ no 'kje ɾe   βi 'βiɾ
no quiere   vivir, no quiere   vivir
not he wants to live not he wants to live

'a
Ah!
Ah!

Poor forgotten *majo*, how hard is
his suffering, suffering, suffering!
since the ungrateful one left him
he will not,
he will not live, he will not live.
Ah!

5
el mi 'ɾar ðe la 'ma xa
El mirar de la maja
The gaze of the *Maja*

por 'ke‿(e)s em mis 'o xos
¿Por qué es   en mis ojos
Why   is it in   my eyes

tan 'on do‿el mi ɾar
tan hondo el   mirar
so   deep   the gaze

ke a 'fin   de kor 'tar
que a fin   de cortar
that in order to cut down

dez 'de nes j‿e 'no xos
desdenes   y   enojos
disdains   and annoyances

los 'swe lo‿en tor 'nar
los   suelo   entornar?
them I used to keep half closed

'ke   'fwe ɣo 'ðen tɾo ʎe βa 'ɾan
¿Qué fuego   dentro llevarán
What fire   inside   they must have

ke   si‿a 'ka so kon ka 'lor
que si acaso   con calor
that if perhaps with heat

¿Por qué es en mis ojos
tan hondo el mirar
que a fin de cortar
desdenes y enojos
los suelo entornar?
¿Qué fuego dentro llevarán
que si acaso con calor
los clavo en mi amor
sonrojo me dan?
Por eso el chispero
a quien mi alma dí
al verse ante mí
me tira el sombrero
y díceme así:
"Mi Maja, no me mires más
que tus ojos rayos son
y ardiendo en pasión
la muerte me dan."

los   'kla βo̯ em mj a 'mor
los   clavo   en mi amor
them I nail   on my lover

son 'ro xo me 'ðan
sonrojo   me dan?
blushing   me they give

poɾ 'e so̯ el   tʃis 'pe ɾo
Por eso   el   chispero
For this   the sparkler

a 'kjem mj 'al ma 'ði
a quien mi alma dí
to whom my soul   I gave

al   'βer se   'an te 'mi
al   verse   ante mí
upon seeing himself before me

me 'ti ɾa   el som 'bɾe ɾo
me tira   el sombrero
me he pulls my hat

i   'ði θe me̯ a 'si
y díceme   así:
and he tells me thus

mi 'ma xa 'no me 'mi ɾes 'mas
"Mi Maja, no me mires más
My Maja   not me look at more

ke tus 'o xos 'ra ɟos 'son
que tus ojos   rayos son
for your eyes   rays   they are

Why do my eyes
have such a deep gaze
that I must keep them half closed
to prevent
feelings of disdain and resentment?
Such fire there must be in them
that if I fix them, perchance,
on my lover
they make me blush.
That is why that sparkle of a man
to whom I gave my soul,
pulls down my hat
when he looks at me,
and says:
"My *Maja*, don't you look at me
no more,
'cause your eyes are lightning
and they kill me with their passion
fire."

j̣ ar 'ðjen do͜ em pa 'sjon
y ardiendo en pasión
and burning   with passion

la 'mwer te me ðan
la muerte me dan.
the death   me they give

6
el 'ma xo 'ti mi ðo
El majo timido
The *majo* shy

'ʎe ɣa   (a) mi 're xa j̣   me 'mi ɾa
Llega   a mi reja y   me mira
He arrives at my grill   and me he looks at

por la 'no tʃe um 'ma xo
por la noche un majo
by   night   a   *majo*

ke͜ en 'kwan to me 'βe j̣ sus 'pi ɾa
que, en cuanto   me ve y suspira,
who as soon as   me he sees and sighs

se 'βa   'ka ʎe a 'βa xo
se va   calle abajo.
he leaves street downward

'aj 'ke 'ti o 'mas tar 'ði o
¡Ay que tío   más tardío!
Oh what a guy more slow

Llega a mi reja y me mira
por la noche un majo
que, en cuanto me ve y suspira,
se va calle abajo.
¡Ay qué tío más tardío!
¡Si así se pasa la vida estoy
divertida!

Si hoy también pasa y me mira
y no se entusiasma
pues le suelto este saludo:
¡Adiós Don Fantasma!
¡Ay que tío más tardío!
¡Odian las enamoradas
las rejas calladas!

——————— • ———————

Every night, a *majo*
comes to my window and looks at
me.
He sees me, he sighs,
and he walks down the street.
What a slow guy!
If this is his style, I'll have to wait
forever!

sj a 'si se 'pa sa   la 'βi ða es 'toj
Si así se pasa   la vida, estoy
If this way he spends his life   I am

ði βer 'ti ða
divertida.
amused

si 'oj   tam 'bjem 'pa sa j   me
Si hoy también pasa y   me
If today also   he passes and me

'mi ɾa
mira
he looks at

i   'no s(e)   en tu 'siaz ma
y   no se   entusiasma
and not himself becomes enthusiastic

'pwes le   'swel to 'es te sa 'lu ðo
pues le   suelto este saludo:
then to him I give this salute:

a 'djoz   doŋ fan 'taz ma
¡Adiós   Don Fantasma!
Goodbye Sir   Ghost!

'aj 'ke 'ti o 'mas tar 'ði o
¡Ay qué tio   más tardío!
Ah what a guy more slow!

'o ðjan las   e na mo 'ɾa ðas
¡Odian las   enamoradas
They hate the women in love

laz 're xas ka 'ʎa ðas
las rejas calladas!
the grills silent!

If today he comes again and looks at me
and he doesn't take the first step,
I'll greet him with:
Hello Mister Ghost!
What a slow guy!
Women in love
hate silent windows!

7

el tra la 'la j el pun te 'a ðo
El tra la la y el punteado
The Tra la la and the staccato

,es em 'bal de 'ma xo 'mi o ke
Es en balde, majo   mío, que
It is in vain   *majo*   mine that

'si ɣas a 'βlan do
sigas hablando
you go on talking

'por ke 'aj 'ko sas   ke   kon 'tes to
porque hay cosas   que contesto
because there are things that I answer

'ɟo 'sjem pɾe kan 'tan do
yo siempre cantando:
I   always   singing

tra la la
Tra la la ...
Tra la la ...

por 'mas ke   pɾe 'ɣun tes 'tan to
Por más que preguntes tanto:
For more that you ask   so much

tra la la
Tra la la ...
Tra la la ...

em 'mi no 'kaw sas ke 'βran to
En mí no causas   quebranto
In me not you cause hurt

Es en balde, majo mío, que sigas
hablando
porque hay cosas que contesto yo
siempre cantando:
Tra la la ...
Por más que preguntes tanto:
tra la la ...
En mí no causas quebranto
ni yo he de salir de mi canto:
tra la la ...

———————— • ————————

It is in vain, my *majo*, to keep on
talking
because there are things that I
always answer with a song:
tra la la ...
No matter how much you ask:
tra la la ...
You cannot distress me
nor will I stop my singing:
tra la la ...

'ni 'ɟo e ðe   sa 'lir ðe   mi
ni yo he de salir de   mi
nor I   have to depart from my

'kan to tra la la
canto: tra la la
singing tra la la

8
la 'ma xa ðe 'ɤo ɟa
La maja de Goya
The *maja* by Goya

'ɟo no (o)l βi ða 're (e)m mi 'βi ða
Yo no olvidaré en mi vida
I   not will forget   in   my life

de 'ɤo ɟa la j 'ma xen ga 'ʎar ða j   ke 'ri ða
de Goya la imagen gallarda y   querida.
by Goya the image   gallant   and loved

no 'aj 'em bra   ni 'ma xa o se 'ɲo ra
No hay hembra ni maja o señora
Not there is female nor *maja*   or lady

ke a 'ɤo ɟa no 'e tʃe ðe me nos a 'o ra
que a Goya no eche de menos ahora.
who to Goya not miss   now

si 'ɟo a 'ʎa ra ˌkjem me a 'ma ra
Si yo hallara quien me amara
If I   found who   me he loved

'ko mo 'el me a 'mo
como él me amó,
like   he me loved

Yo no olvidaré en mi vida
de Goya la imagen gallarda y
querida.
No hay hembra ni maja o señora
que a Goya no eche de menos
ahora.

So yo hallara quien me amara
como él me amó,
no envidiara ni anhelara más
venturas ni dichas yo,
no envidiara ni anhelara más
venturas ni dichas yo.

———————————●———

I will never forget
Goya's gallant and dear appearance.
There is no woman, neither *maja*
nor lady,
who does not miss Goya now.

If I found one who would love me
as he did,
I would not envy anyone, I could
not desire more happiness,
I would not envy anyone, I could
not desire more happiness.

no em bi 'ðja ɾa ni   a ne 'la ɾa
no envidiara   ni   anhelara
not would I envy nor would I desire

'maz ben 'tu ɾa, ni 'ði tjas 'ɟo
más venturas   ni dichas yo,
more happiness or joys   I

no em bi 'ðja ɾa ni   a ne 'la ɾa
no envidiara   ni   anhelara
not would I envy nor would I desire

'maz ben 'tu ɾas, ni 'ði tjas 'ɟo
más venturas   ni dichas yo,
more happiness   or joys   I

9
la 'ma xa ðo lo 'ɾo sa
La maja dolorosa No. 1
The *maja* sorrowful

o   'mwer te 'kɾwel
¡Oh muerte   cruel!
Oh death   cruel

por 'ke   'tu a tɾaj 'θjon
¿Por qué tú, a traición,
Why   you in treason

mi 'ma xo a re βa 'tas te a   ,mi pa 'sjon
mi majo   arrebataste a   mi pasión?
my *majo*   you dislodged from my passion

no 'kje ɾo βi 'βir sin 'el
¡No quiero vivir sin él,
Not I want to live without him

¡Oh muerte cruel!
¿Por qué tú, a traición,
mi majo arrebataste a mi pasión?
¡No quiero vivir sin él,
porque es morir, porque es morir
así vivir!

No es posible ya
sentir más dolor:
en lágrimas desecha ya mi alma
está.
¡Oh Dios, torna mi amor,
porque es morir, porque es morir
así vivir!

por k(e) 'es mo 'riɾ por k(e) 'es
porque es morir, porque es
because it is dying because it is
mo 'riɾ a 'si ßi 'ßir
morir así vivir!
dying thus to live

no 'es   po 'si ßle 'ja
No es   posible ya
Not it is possible now

sen 'tir 'maz do 'loɾ
sentir más dolor:
to feel more pain

en 'la ɣri maz de 'se tʃa 'ja   mi 'al ma es 'ta
en lágrimas desecha ya   mi alma está.
in tears   broken   now my soul   is

o   'ðjos 'tor na mi a 'mor
¡Oh Dios, torna   mi amor;
Oh God return my love

por k(e) 'es mo 'riɾ por k(e) 'es mo 'riɾ
porque es morir, porque es morir
because it is dying because it is dying
a 'si ßi 'ßir
así vivir!
thus to live

Oh cruel death!
Why did you treacherously
remove my *majo* from my life?
I do not want to live without him.
For to live this way
is to die, is to die!

It is no longer possible
to feel more sorrow:
my soul lies broken up in tears.
Oh God! Return my lover to me
for to live this way
is to die, is to die!

10
La maja dolorosa No. 2

'aj   'ma xo ðe mi 'βi ða
¡Ay majo   de mi vida,
Oh *majo*   of my life

'no 'no 'tu no‿as   'mwer to
no, no, tú no has   muerto!
no, no   you not have died

a 'ka so   'ɟo‿e sis 'tje se
¿Acaso   yo existiese
Perchance I   would exist

si 'fwe ɾa‿'e so 'θjer to
si fuera eso   cierto?
if it was this   true

'kje ɾo   'lo ka βe 'sar tu 'βo ka
¡Quiero, loca, besar tu boca!
I want   crazed to kiss your mouth

'kje ɾo   se 'ɣu ɾa ɣo 'θar 'maz de
Quiero, segura,   gozar más de
I want   safe   to enjoy more
tu βen 'tu ɾa
tu ventura,
your fortune

'aj ðe   tu βen 'tu ɾa
¡ay!, de tu ventura.
oh   your fortune

¡Ay majo de mi vida,
no, no, tú no has muerto!
¿Acaso yo existiese
si fuera eso cierto?
¡Quiero, loca, besar tu boca!
Quiero, segura, gozar más de tu
ventura,
¡ay!, de tu ventura.

Mas, ¡ay!, deliro, sueño:
mi majo no existe.
En torno mío el mundo
lloroso está y triste.
¡A mi duelo no hallo consuelo!
Mas muerto y frío siempre el majo
será mío.
¡Ay! Siempre mío.

———————•———————

Oh, *majo* of my life,
no, no, you are not dead.
Could I still be alive
if that were true?
Like a crazed woman, I want to
kiss your mouth.
I want the comfort of enjoying
your happiness,
oh, your happiness.

But, oh!, I am delirious, I dream:
my *majo* is no longer.
The world all around me
is sad, in tears.
There is no comfort for my
sorrow!
But dead and cold the *majo* will
always be mine,
oh!, always mine.

mas 'aj   ðe 'li ɾo 'swe ɲo
Mas, ¡ay!, deliro, sueño:
But oh   I am delirious I dream

mi 'ma xo no e̯ 'sis te
mi majo   no existe.
my *majo*   not he exists

en 'tor no 'mi o̯ e̯l   'mun do
En torno mío   el   mundo
Around   me   the world

ʎo 'ro so̯ es 'ta j̯   'tris te
lloroso   está   y   triste.
tearful   it is   and sad

a   mi 'ðwe lo   no̯ 'a ʎo kon 'swe lo
¡A   mi duelo   no   hallo consuelo!
For my mourning not I find consolation

maz 'mwer to̯ j̯ 'fɾi o   'sjeɱ pɾ(e) e̯l
Mas muerto   y frío,   siempre   el
But dead   and cold forever   the
'ma xo se 'ɾa   'mi o
majo   será   mío.
majo   will be mine

'aj   'sjeɱ pɾe 'mi o
¡ay! Siempre mío.
oh, forever   mine

11
La maja dolorosa No. 3

de̯ a 'kel 'ma xo̯ a 'man te ke 'fwe
De aquel majo amante que fue
Of that *majo* lover who was

mi 'ɣlo rja
mi gloria
my glory

'gwar ðo̯ a ne'lan te ði 'tʃo sa me 'mo rja
guardo anhelante dichosa memoria.
I keep eagerly a happy memory

'el me̯ a ðo 'ra βa βe: 'men te j 'fjel
El me adoraba vehemente y fiel.
He me adored with vehemence and faith

'ɟo mi 'βi ða̯ e̩n 'te ɾa 'ði a 'el
Yo mi vida entera di a él.
I my life whole gave to him

j 'o tras ˌmil 'dje ɾa si 'el
Y otras mil diera si él
And other thousand I would give if he

ki 'sje ɾa
quisiera,
wanted

ke (e)n 'on dos a 'mo ɾez mar 'ti ɾjos 'son
que en hondos amores martirios son
for in deep loves torments are

las 'flo ɾes
las flores.
the flowers

De aquel majo amante
que fue mi gloria
guardo anhelante
dichosa memoria.
El me adoraba
vehemente y fiel.
Yo mi vida entera
di a él.
Y otras mil diera
si él quisiera,
que en hondos amores
martirios son las flores.

Y al recordar mi majo amado
van resurgiendo ensueños
de un tiempo pasado.

Ni en el Mentidero
ni en la Florida
majo más majo
paseó en la vida.
Bajo el chambergo
sus ojos ví
con toda el alma
puestos en mí.
Que a quien miraban
enamoraban,
pues no hallé en el mundo
mirar más profundo.

Y al recordar mi majo amado
van resurgiendo ensueños
de un tiempo pasado.

j al   re koɾ 'ðaɾ   mi 'ma xo̯ a 'ma ðo
Y al   recordar   mi majo amado
And when remembering my *majo* loved

'ban   re suɾ 'xjen do̯ en 'swe ɲos
van   resurgiendo   ensueños
they are re-emerging   reveries

de̯ un 'tjeŋ po pa 'sa ðo
de un tiempo pasado.
from a   time   past

nj   en el men ti 'ðe ɾo nj̯ en la
Ni   en el Mentidero ni én la
Neither in the Mentidero   nor in the
flo 'ɾi ða
Florida
Florida

'ma xo 'maz 'ma xo pa 'sjo̯ en la 'βi ða
majo más majo   paseó en la vida.
majo prettier   walked in life [ever]

'ba xo̯ el tʃam 'ber ɣo sus 'o xoz 'bi
Bajo el chambergo sus ojos ví
Under the hat   his eyes I saw

kon 'to ða̯ el 'al ma 'pwes tos em 'mi
con toda el alma puestos en   mí.
with all   his soul   fixed   upon me

ˌke a 'kjen   mi 'ra βan
Que a quien   miraban
that to whomever they looked
e na mo 'ra βan
enamoraban,
they enamored

I eagerly keep a happy memory.
Of that loving *majo* who was my joy.
He adored me, passionate and faithful.
I gave him my whole life.
And I would have given him a thousand more lives
if he had wanted them,
for sacrifice is the flower of the deepest love.

Reveries come to me from a time past
When I now remember my beloved *majo*.

I never saw a more handsome *majo* walking down the street or going to church.
I saw, under his hat, his eyes fixed upon me with all their might;
all who would see them would fall in love with him,
for never in the whole world did I see a deeper gaze.

Reveries come to me from a time past
When I now remember my beloved *majo*.

'pwes no‿a 'ʎe‿ (e)n el 'mun do
pues no hallé en el mundo
because not I found in the world

mi 'ɾar 'mas pɾo 'fun do
miraɾ más profundo.
a gaze more profound

j‿ al re koɾ 'ðaɾ mi 'ma xo‿a 'ma ðo
Y al recordar mi majo amado
And when remembering my *majo* loved

'ban re suɾ 'xjen do‿en 'swe ɲos
van resurgiendo ensueños
they are re-emerging reveries

de‿ un 'tjeŋ po pa 'sa ðo
de un tiempo pasado.
from a time past

12
las ku ru 'ta kas mo 'ðes tas
Las currutacas modestas
The fashion-conscious modest [women]

de 'θið 'ke ða mi 'se las se 'βen
Decid qué damiselas se ven
Tell [me] what damsels one sees

poɾ a 'i
por ahí
around here

ke 'luθ kan a 'si
que luzcan así.
who shine thus

Decid qué damiselas se ven por ahí
que luzcan así.
Al vernos a las dos no hay quien
no diga:
Dios que os bendiga.

Porque hace falta ver
el invencible poder
de que goza una mujer
cerca nacida de la Moncloa o la
Florida.

al 'βer nos a laz 'dos no‿'aj ˌkjen
Al vernos a las dos no hay quien
When seeing the two not there is who
no 'ði ɣa
no diga:
not say

'djos ke‿os βen 'di ɣa
Dios que os bendiga.
God that you He may bless

poɾ ke‿'a θe 'fal ta 'βeɾ
Porque hace falta ver
Because there is need to see

el im ben 'θi βle po 'ðer
el invencible poder
the invincible power

de ke 'ɣo θa‿u na mu 'xer
de que goza una mujer
of which she enjoys a woman

'θer ka na 'θi ða ðe la mon 'klo a‿o la
cerca nacida de la Moncloa o la
near born to the Moncloa or the
flo 'ri ða
Florida.
Florida

'pwes 'di ɣa‿us 'te
Pues diga usté
Well you say you

Pues diga usté
si en tierra alguna viose otro pie
tan requetechiquito, ¡olé!

Y pues nuestra abuela muriese
tiempo ha,
toda modestia sobra ya. ¡Ja, ja!

———————— • ————————

Tell me what damsels there are to
see
As elegant as we.
When anyone sees the two of us
he will say:
May the Lord bless you!

For it is wondrous to see
The invincible power
of women born near Moncloa or
Florida.

So tell me if you have seen,
anywhere else in the world,
feet as tiny as ours. Olé!

Since our grandmothers died a
long time ago
we can no longer be modest. Ha!

sj en 'tje r(a) al 'gu na 'βjo se 'o tɾo
si en tierra   alguna   viose   otro
if on land   any   one saw another

'pje
pie
foot

tan re ke ˌte tʃi 'ki to o 'le
tan requetechiquito. ¡Olé!
so   extra-very tiny   Ole!

i   'pwes 'nwes tɾ(a) a 'βwe la mu 'ɾje se
Y   pues nuestra   abuela muriese
And since   our   grandmother died

'tjeŋ po 'a
tiempo ha,
time ago

'to ða mo 'ðes tja 'so βɾa 'ʝa   xa 'xa
toda   modestia   sobra ya.   ¡Ja, ja!
any   modesty   is superfluous now Ha, ha!

II. *Canciones españolas*

"Si al Retiro me llevas" (If You Take Me to the Retiro)
"Canto gitano" (Gypsy Song)

Jealousy and cuckoldry are two important motifs in Spanish popular culture. The *tonadilla* "Si al Retiro me llevas…" is spoken by a woman as a warning to her husband. The Retiro is the most famous park in Madrid; it is to this day a favorite place for a late afternoon stroll, and also for flirting and courting. The park is usually full of young men; the text of the song uses a singular *tanto galán* with a plural meaning, as is common in Spanish. The whole song has the light air of popular culture; its subject matter is accordingly piquant. The lady suggests that she may find a lover in the park, since her husband fails to keep her locked up as one would a jewel. If she were to become unfaithful her husband would, according to the old metaphor for cuckoldry, grow horns—hence her reference to "a pain in the forehead."

We have transcribed the *Canto gitano* according to the pronunciation of Andalusian Spanish since the song is located in an idealized setting populated by gypsies, presumably near Granada or in some other mountain location in Andalusia. The use of the word *serrana* ('girl from the *sierra*' or 'mountain range') makes this clear. Also, since the Middle Ages, *serrana* has been the autochthonous Spanish term equivalent to the French *pastourelle*. Like the *majos* in the *Colección de tonadillas*, the gypsies are favorite inhabitants of the idyllic world of song.

13
sj al re 'ti ɾo me 'ʎe βas
Si al Retiro me llevas
If to the Retiro me you take

sj al   re 'ti ɾo   me 'ʎe βas
Si al   **Retiro**   **me llevas**
If to the Retiro   me you take

'en tɾe 'tan to   ɣa 'lan
entre tanto   **galán,**
among so many young men

por la   'no tʃe no 'ði ɣas
por la   **noche no**   **digas**
by [the] night   do not say

ke   te   'sjen tes 'muj 'mal
que te   **sientes muy mal.**
that you feel   very bad

ke l   ma 'ɾi   ðo   ke n 'se ɲa
Que el   **marido que enseña**
For the husband who shows

la ke   'ðe βe   ɣwar 'ðaɾ
la que debe   **guardar,**
she who he must keep in

no 'es es 'tɾa   ɲo ke 'ði ɣa
no es extraño   **que diga**
not it is strange that he says

ke   le 'ðwe le l   fɾon 'tal
que le duele   **el frontal.**
that to him it hurts the forehead.

Si al Retiro me llevas
entre tanto galán,
por la noche no digas
que te sientes muy mal.
Que el marido que enseña
la que debe guardar,
no es extraño que diga
que le duele el frontal.

———————— • ————————

If you take me to the Retiro
amidst so many gallant young men,
do not say, when nighttime comes,
that you feel very bad.
For a husband who shows off
her who should be kept in,
may easily complain
of a pain in his forehead.

14
'kan to xi 'ta no
Canto gitano
Song gypsy

'aj ma ðɾe 'si ta	ðe mis en 'tɾa ɲas
¡Ay madrecita	**de mis entrañas,**
O, dear mother	of my entrails

me 'an	ro'βao a mi xi 'ta na
me han	**robao a mi gitana!**
me they have stolen	my gypsy girl

me	'poŋ go	'tris te	'ma ðɾe	ðel	'əl ma
Me	**pongo**	**triste,**	**madre**	**del**	**alma**
myself I get	sad	mother	of the soul		

'por ke	'pjer ðo mi	se 'ra na
porque pierdo	**mi serrana.**
because I lose	my *serrana*

se ra 'ni ka	ðe mi 'βi ða
Serranica	**de mi vida.**
Little *serrana* of my life

a 'ti no te 'ðwe	le l 'ɑl ma
A ti no te duele	**el alma.**
To you not it hurts the	soul

'aj ma ðɾe 'si ta	ðe mis en 'tɾa ɲas
¡Ay madrecita	**de mis entrañas,**
O dear mother	of my entrails

¡Ay madrecita de mis entrañas,
me han robao a mi gitana!
Me pongo triste, madre del alma
porque pierdo mi serrana.

Serranica de mi vida,
a ti no te duele el alma.
¡Ay madrecita de mis entrañas,
me han robao a mi gitana!

¡Ay madrecita de mis entrañas,
yo no sé lo que me pasa!
Sin mi chiquilla me vuelvo loco,
y el corazón se me abrasa.

Serranica de mi vida,
el tuyo no siente nada.
¡Ay madrecita de mis entrañas,
me han robao a mi gitana!

———————————— • ————————————

Oh dear mother of my heart,
They have stolen my gypsy girl!
I am sad, dear mother,
For I have lost the one I love.

Gypsy girl of my life,
Your soul is not hurting.
Oh dear mother of my heart,
They have stolen my gypsy girl!

me‿'an   ro'βao̯‿a mi xi 'ta na
me han   robao a mi gitana!
me they have stolen   my gypsy girl

Oh dear mother of my heart,
I don't know what's happened to me!
Without my girl I go crazy
And my heart is on fire.

'ʝo no 'se   lo ke   me 'pa sa
Yo no sé   lo que   me pasa!
I   not know that which to me happens

Gypsy girl of my life,
Your heart is feeling nothing.
Oh dear mother of my heart,
They have stolen my gypsy girl!

͵sim‿mi   tʃi 'ki ʎa   me βwel bo 'lo ko
Sin mi   chiquilla   me vuelvo loco,
Without my little girl   I   turn   crazy

j‿el   ko ɾa 'son se me‿a̯ 'βɾa sa
y el   corazón   se me abrasa.
and the heart   to me it burns

Se ɾa 'ni ka ðe mi 'bi ða
Serranica   de mi vida.
Little *serrana* of my life

el   'tu ʝo no   'sjen te 'na ða]
El   tuyo no   siente nada.
The (heart of) yours does not feel anything

'aj ma ðɾe 'si ta   ðe mis en 'tɾa ɲas
¡Ay madrecita   de mis entrañas,
O dear mother   of my entrails

me‿'an   ro'βao̯‿a mi xi 'ta na
me han   robao a mi gitana!
me they have stolen   my gypsy girl

III. *Canciones amatorias*

(*Love Songs*)

"Descúbrase el pensamiento de mi secreto cuidado" (Let Me Unveil the Thoughts of My Secret Love)
"Mañanica era" (It Was Midsummer Morning)
"Llorad, Corazón, que tenéis razón" (Cry, My Heart, for You Have a Reason)
"Mira que soy niña, iamor, déjame!" (I Am but a Girl, My Love)
"No lloréis ojuelos" (Don't Cry, Little Eyes)
"Iban al pinar" (They Went to the Pine Grove)
"Gracia Mía" (My Gracious One)

The theme of love unites, very generally, these seven songs. In style they fall into two broad categories (we might call them respectively European and Spanish, as the following paragraphs will make explicit. These are mostly songs with a strong basis in folklore, although all have been rewritten by a modern, professional hand, which remains nevertheless anonymous.

Songs three and seven were dedicated by the composer to one of his favorite interpreters, the Catalan soprano Concepció Badia (Barcelona, 1897).

Even though "Descúbrase" is a modern song, it contains remnants of the medieval troubadour tradition. Love, according to that tradition and to this song, is a service from the lover, who is also the speaker of the poem, to a Lady who is superior to him. The twelfth-century troubadours from southern France may have developed this archetypal situation as a metaphor for feudal vassalage. What is left nowadays is the veneration of the woman who, through her beauty, holds a kind of passive power over the lover. A situation of this nature almost begs for the lady's indifference or neglect. It is an even older tradition that eyesight is the first cause of love.

"Mañanica era" goes several steps further in the direction pointed to by the previous song. The lady has become the goddess of love, Venus; the lover, not unhappy enough with his unrequited service, prepares to die of love. The opening lines refer to midsummer morning, a Christianization of the pagan celebration of the summer solstice in the feast of Saint John. Several well-known Spanish ballads relate mysterious love deeds taking place on that sacred date.

"Llorad, corazón" presents a more traditionally Spanish alternative to the love story. Here the sufferer (for it seems that love is always suffering) is the woman. The noun referring to her is *niña*, which literally means 'child girl'; one assumes, however, that the song alludes to an adult woman's first love and not to any premature sexual experience.

The next song, "Mira que soy niña," is related to the one preceding it. The *niña* here expresses a coy prudence; but by her repeated exclamations she shows that she is truly experiencing love, since she uses the verb 'to die' as if she were both ready and afraid to go to the end of the experience.

In "No lloréis," a very simple poem, we see a characteristic Spanish taste for antithesis: jealousy-love, laughter-tears.

The word *serranas*, so crucial in the song "Iban al pinar," is related to the word *sierra* or 'mountain range' and means what our translation says quite literally. It is also a term loaded with literary significance, dating back to the Middle Ages. The Provençal troubadours developed a type of love poem in which a traveling knight finds a shepherd girl alone in the fields and tries to seduce her. These poems were called *pastorellas* from the Provençal word for shepherdess. In the Spanish versions of the *pastorellas*, however, the woman is always referred to as *serrana* or in the diminutive *serranilla*. This song is surely derived from some traditional rhythm developed to accompany or celebrate the pine-nut harvest, a very labor-intensive crop as the reader can imagine. The poem seems to be a learned elaboration of the traditional rhythm, since we find direct references to Cupid, the "blind god," and to the arrows from his bow that cause people to fall in love. The *serranas* from the Castilian region of Cuenca, both the hard-working ones and those who prefer to dance, are so beautiful that they can ridicule even Cupid after he has borrowed Apollo's eyes to peep on them.

The Spanish word *gracia* has a wide range of meanings, from the 'grace' of God, to 'gratefulness', to 'jocularity'. *Tener gracia*, 'to have grace', means both to be funny and to be graceful. *Gracia* is a concept comparable to that of 'charisma'. In the last song of the cycle, "Gracia mía", we return to some courtly archetypes: The lady, who is the singer's *gracia*, holds such power that the singer may get lost, that is, die of love. We notice once again the taste for antithesis: *perder*, 'to lose', is coupled both with *hallar*, 'to find', and with *ganar*, 'to win'.

15

des 'ku βra se‿(e)l pen sa 'mjen to ðe mi se 'kɾe to kwj 'ða ðo

Descúbrase el pensamiento de mi secreto cuidado

Let it be unveiled the thought of my secret love

des 'ku βra se⌣(e)l pen sa 'mjen to ðe
Descúbrase   el   pensamiento   de
Let it be unveiled the thought   of
mi se 'kɾe to kuj 'ða ðo
mi secreto   cuidado,
my secret   love

'pwes des ku 'βrir miz ðo 'lo ɾes mi
pues descubrir   mis dolores, mi
and   unveil   my sufferings my
βi 'βiɾ a pa sjo 'na ðo
vivir apasionado;
living passionate

Descúbrase el pensamiento
de mi secreto cuidado,
pues descubrir mis dolores,
mi vivir apasionado;
no es de agora mi pasión,
días ha que soy penado.
Una señora a quien sirvo
mi servir tiene olvidado,
mi servir tiene olvidado.

Su beldad me hizo suyo,
el su gesto tan pulido
en mi alma está esmaltado.
¡Ah! ¡Ay de mí!
Que la miré, que la miré
para vivir lastimado,
para llorar y plañir
glorias del tiempo pasado.
¡Ah! Mi servir tiene olvidado.

———————— • ————————

'no̯ ez ðe̯a 'ɣo ɾa mi pa 'sjon 'di as
no es de agora mi pasíon, días
not it is from now my passion days

'a ke 'soj pe 'na ðo
ha que soy penado.
it's been that I am in pain.

'u na se 'ɲo ɾa (a) 'kjen 'sir βo
Una señora a quien sirvo
One lady to whom I serve

mi ser 'βiɾ 'tje ne̯ol βi 'ða ðo
mi servir tiene olvidado,
my service has forgotten

mi ser 'βiɾ 'tje ne̯ol βi 'ða ðo
mi servir tiene olvidado.
my service has forgotten

su βel 'dað me̯'i θo 'su ʝo
Su beldad me hizo suyo,
Her beauty me it made hers

el su 'xes to tan pu 'li ðo̯em mi̯
el su gesto tan pulido en mi
the her gesture so pretty in my

'al ma̯es 'ta̯z mal 'ta ðo
alma está esmaltado.
soul it is engraved

'a 'aj ðe 'mi
¡Ah! ¡Ay de mí!
Ah! Woe [is] me

ke la mi 'ɾe
Que la miré,
who her I looked at

ke la mi 'ɾe
que la miré,
who her I looked at

Let me unveil the thoughts
of my secret love,
and reveal my sorrows,
my impassioned life;
my passion is not new,
I have suffered for many days now.
A lady whom I serve,
has forgotten my service,
has forgotten my service.

Her beauty made me hers,
her elegance in movement
is engraved on my soul.
Ah! Woe is me,
who looked at her, who looked at her
only to live in sorrow,
to weep and to lament
the glories of time past.
Ah! She has forgotten my service.

'pa ɾa   βi 'βir las ti 'ma ðo
para   vivir   lastimado,
in order to live wounded

'pa ɾa   ʎo 'ɾaɾ i   pla 'ɲir   'ɣlo ɾjaz
para   llorar   y   plañir   glorias
in order to cry   and to lament glories
ðel   'tjem po pa 'sa ðo
del   tiempo   pasado.
from time   past

'a   mi ser 'βiɾ 'tje ne‿ol βi 'ða ðo
¡Ah! mi servir   tiene   olvidado.
Ah! my service   has   forgotten

16
ma ɲa 'ni ka 'e ɾa
Mañanica era
Little morning it was

ma ɲa 'ni ka 'eɾa   ma 'ɲa na ðe
Mañanica   era,   mañana   de
Little morning it was morning   of
saŋ 'xwan   se ðe 'θi a‿(a)l 'fin
san Juan   se decía   al fin,
Saint John's   it was said at last

'kwan do‿a 'ke ʎa   'ðjo sa   'βe nus
cuando   aquella diosa   Venus
when   that   goddess Venus
'den tɾo ðe‿um 'fɾes ko xar 'ðin,
dentro de un fresco   jardín
inside   a fresh   garden

to 'man do‿es 'ta ßa la 'fres ka‿(a) la
tomando estaba la fresca a la
taking she was the fresh [air] in the

'som ßra ðe‿uŋ xaθ 'min
sombra de un jazmín
shade of a jasmine

ka 'ße ʎos en su ka 'ße θa pa ɾe 'θi a‿un
cabellos en su cabeza, parecía un
hairs on her head she seemed a

se ɾa 'fin
serafín.
seraph

sus me 'xi ʎas i sus 'la ßjos 'ko mo
Sus mejillas y sus labios como
Her cheeks and her lips like

ko 'lor ðe ru 'ßi
color de rubí
color of ruby

j‿el op 'xeto ðe su 'ka ɾa fi ɣu 'ɾa ßa‿uŋ
y el objeto de su cara figuraba un
and the object of her face seemed a

ke ɾu 'ßin
querubín;
cherub

a 'ʎi ðe 'flo ɾes flo 'ɾi ðas a 'θi a‿un
allí de flores floridas hacía un
there of flowers flowered she made a

'ri ko ko 'xin
rico cojín,
rich cushion

Mañanica era, mañana
de San Juan se decía al fin,
cuando aquella diosa Venus
dentro de un fresco jardín
tomando estaba la fresca
a la sombra de un jazmín,
cabellos en su cabeza,
parecía un serafín.
Sus mejillas y sus labios
como color de rubí
y el objeto de su cara
figuraba un querubín;
allí de flores floridas
hacía un rico cojín,
de rosas una guirnalda
para el que venía a morir,
¡ah!, lentamente por amores
sin a nadie descubrir.

———————— • ————————

It was midsummer morning, the morning
of Saint John's, at last,
when the goddess Venus
in her cool garden
was enjoying the coolness
in the shade of a jasmine bush.
With her hair on her head
she looked like a seraph.
Her cheeks and her lips
were the color of rubies
and all her countenance
seemed one of a cherub;
there out of flowering bouquets
she was making a fancy cushion,
and a garland of roses
for one who came to die,
ah, a slow death for a love
he would reveal to no one.

de 'ro sas una ɣir 'nal ða
de rosas   una guirnalda
of roses   a   garland
'pa ɾa̬ el ke βe 'ni a̬ (a) mo 'ɾiɾ
para el que venía a morir,
for he who came to die

'a ˌlen ta 'men te poɾ   a 'mo ɾes
¡ah!, lentamente   por   amores
ah   slowly   because of love
sin a 'na ðje   ðes ku 'βɾiɾ
sin a nadie   descubrir.
without to anyone discovering [it]

17
ʎo 'ɾað ko ɾa 'θoŋ ke te 'nejs ra 'θon
Llorad, Corazón, que tenéis razón
Cry, heart, for you have reason

ʎo 'ɾa βa la 'ni ɲa̬ j   te 'ni a ɾa 'θon
Lloraba la niña, y   tenía   razón,
Cried   the girl and she had reason

la pɾo 'li xa̬ (a)w 'sen θja
la prolija   ausencia
the prolix   absence
ðe su jŋ 'gɾa to̬ a 'mor
de su ingrato   amor,
of her ungrateful love
ðe su jŋ 'gɾa to̬ a' mor
de su ingrato   amor,
of her ungrateful love

Lloraba la niña, y tenía razón,
la prolija ausencia de su ingrato
amor, de su ingrato amor.
Dejola tan niña que apenas, creo
yo,
que tenía los años que ha que la
dejó.
Llorando la ausencia del galán
traidor:
la halla la luna y la deja el sol,
añadiendo siempre pasión a pasión,
memoria a memoria, dolor a dolor,
dolor a dolor.
Llorad, corazón, que tenéis razón.

de 'xo la tan   'ni ɲa ke   a 'pe nas
Dejola tan   niña   que apenas,
He left her so girl   that barely

'kɾe o 'ʝo
creo yo,
I believe

ke   te 'ni a   los 'a ɲos
que tenía   los años
that she had   the years

ke ‿'a   ke   la   ðe 'xo
que ha   que la   dejó.
that it's been since her he left

ʎo 'ran do la ‿(a)w 'sen θja
Llorando la ausencia
crying (for) the absence

ðel ɣa 'lan   tɾaj 'ðor
del galán   traidor:
of the young man treacherous

l(a) 'a ʎa la   'lu na j   la
la halla la   luna y   la
her finds the   moon and her

'ðe xa el   'sol
deja el   sol
leaves the sun

a ɲa 'djen do   'sjem pɾe pa 'sjon a   pa 'sjon
añadiendo   siempre pasión a   pasión
adding   always   passion to passion

The girl was crying, and for a good reason:
the lengthy absence of her ungrateful lover, her ungrateful lover.
He left her so young that, I think, she was then about half as old as she is now.
The moon finds her, and the sun leaves her
crying for the absence of the treacherous gallant:
always adding passion to passion, memory to memory, pain to pain, pain to pain.
Cry, my heart, for you have a reason.

me 'mo ɾja͜ (a) me 'moɾja
memoria   a   memoria,
memory   to memory
ðo 'loɾ a ðo 'loɾ ðo 'loɾ a ðo 'loɾ
dolor a dolor, dolor a dolor.
pain   to pain   pain   to pain

ʎo 'ɾað ko ɾa 'θoŋ ke te 'nejs ɾa 'θon
Llorad, corazón,   que tenéis   razón.
Cry   heart   for you have reason

18
'mi ɾa ke 'soj 'ni ɲa͜ a 'mor 'ðe xa ˌme
Mira que soy niña, ¡amor, déjame!
Look that I am girl, love, leave me

'mi ɾa ke   'soj 'ni ɲa͜ a 'mor
Mira que soy   niña, ¡amor,
Look that I am [a] girl love
'ðe xa ˌme
déjame!
leave me [alone]

'aj   'aj   'aj ke me   mo ɾi 'ɾe
¡Ay!, ¡ay!, ¡ay! que me moriré.
Ah,   ah,   ah! that   I shall die

'pa so͜ a 'mor no 'se as a mi
Paso, amor, no seas   a mi
Slow love   not be   to my
'ɣus to͜ es 'tɾa ɲo
gusto   extraño,
pleasure inimical

Mira que soy niña, ¡amor, déjame!
¡Ay!, ¡ay!, ¡ay!, que me moriré.
Paso, amor, no seas a mi gusto
extraño,
no quieras mi daño
pues mi bien deseas;
basta que me veas
sin llegárteme.
¡Ay!, ¡ay!, ¡ay!, que me moriré.

No seas agora, por ser atrevido;
sé agradecido
con la que te adora,
que así se desdora
mi amor y tu fe.
¡Ay!, ¡ay!, ¡ay!, que me moriré.

no 'kje ɾas   mi 'ða ɲo
no quieras   mi daño
not you want my damage

pwes mi 'βjen de 'se as
pues mi bien deseas;
since my good you wish

'bas ta ke   me 'βe as
basta que   me veas
it suffices that me you see

sin   ʎe 'ɣar te ˌme
sin   llegárteme.
without coming closer to me

'aj   'aj   'aj ke me   mo ɾi 're
¡Ay!, ¡ay!, ¡ay! que me   moriré.
Ah, ah, ah! that   I shall die

no   'se as a 'ɣo ɾa por 'seɾ a tɾe 'βi ðo
No seas   agora,   por ser atrevido;
Not be   now   for being daring

'se a̱ ɣɾa ðe 'θi ðo
sé agradecido
be grateful

ˌkon la ke   te̱ a 'ðo ɾa
con la que te   adora
with she who you adores

ke̱ a 'si se   ðez 'ðo ɾa
que así se   desdora
for thus itself unglitters

Mira que soy niña, ¡amor, déjame!
¡Ay!, ¡ay!, ¡ay!, que me moriré.
Paso, amor, no seas a mi gusto
extraño,
no quieras mi daño
pues mi bien deseas;
basta que me veas
sin llegárteme.
¡Ay!, ¡ay!, ¡ay!, que me moriré.

———————— • ————————

I am but a girl, my love, do not
touch me.
Ah, ah, ah! I shall die.
Easy, love, do not destroy my
pleasure,
do not give me pain
if you want my joy;
just come look at me
but don't get too close.
Ah, ah, ah! I shall die.

Don't be daring now;
be grateful
to the one who adores you
and do not spoil my love or your
faith.
Ah, ah, ah! I shall die.

I am but a girl, my love, do not
touch me.
Ah, ah, ah! I shall die.
Easy, love, do not destroy my
pleasure,
do not give me pain
if you want my joy;
just come look at me
but don't get too close.
Ah, ah, ah! I shall die.

mi‿a 'moɾ i   tu 'fe
mi amor   y   tu fe.
my love   and your faith

'aj   'aj   'aj ke me   mo ɾi 'ɾe
¡Ay!, ¡ay!, ¡ay! que me moriré.
Ah,   ah,   ah! that   I shall die

'mi ɾa ke   'soj 'ni ɲa‿a 'mor
Mira que soy niña, ¡amor,
Look that I am [a] girl love
'ðe xaˌme
déjame!
leave me [alone]

'aj   'aj   'aj ke me   mo ɾi 'ɾe
¡Ay!, ¡ay!, ¡ay! que me moriré.
Ah,   ah,   ah! that   I shall die

'pa so‿a 'mor no 'se as a mi
Paso, amor, no seas a mi
Slow   love   not be   to my
'ɣus to‿es 'tɾa ɲo
gusto   extraño,
pleasure inimical

no 'kje ɾas   mi 'ða ɲo
no quieras mi daño
not you want my damage

pwes mi 'βjen de 'se as
pues mi bien deseas;
since my good you wish

'bas ta ke   me 'β̞e as
basta que   me veas
it suffices that me you see

sin   ʎe 'ɣar te ˌme
sin   llegárteme.
without coming closer to me

'aj   'aj   'aj ke me mo ɾi 'ɾe
¡Ay!, ¡ay!, ¡ay! que me moriré.
Ah, ah, ah! that   I shall die

19
ˌno ʎo 'ɾejs o 'xwe los
No lloréis ojuelos
Not you cry little eyes

ˌno ʎo 'ɾejs o 'xwe los 'por ke 'no̯ ez
No lloréis, ojuelos,   porque no es
Not you cry little eyes because not it is
ra 'θon
razón
reason

ke 'ʎo ɾe ðe 'θe los   kjem 'ma ta
que llore de celos   quien mata
that cry   out of jealousy who   kills
ðe̯ a 'mor
de amor.
out of love

No lloréis, ojuelos,
porque no es razón
que llore de celos
quien mata de amor.

Quien puede matar
no intente morir,
si hace con reir
más que con llorar.

No lloréis, ojuelos,
porque no es razón
que llore de celos
quien mata de amor.

———————— • ————————

Don't cry, little eyes,
it is not fair
for one who can kill with her love
to be crying in jealousy.

kjem   'pwe ðe ma 'tar no̯in 'ten te
Quien puede   matar   no intente
Who   can   kill   not should try

mo 'ɾir
morir,
to die

She who can kill
should not try to die,
if she can do more with laughter
than with tears.

si̯'a θe   kon re' ir   'mas ke
si hace   con reir   más que
if she does with laughing more than

kon ʎo 'ɾar
con llorar.
with crying.

Don't cry, little eyes,
it is not fair
for one who can kill with her love
to be crying in jealousy.

ˌno ʎo 'ɾejs o 'xwe los 'por ke 'no̯ez
No lloréis, ojuelos,   porque no es
Not you cry little eyes because not it is

ra 'θon
razón
reason

ke   'ʎo ɾe ðe 'θe los   kjem 'ma ta
que llore de celos   quien mata
that cry   out of jealousy who   kills

ðe̯a 'mor
de amor.
out of love

20
'i βan al pi 'naɾ
Iban al pinar
They went to the pine grove

se 'ra naz   ðe   'kweŋ ka 'i βan al
Serranas   de   Cuenca   iban   al
Mountain girls from Cuenca   went   to the
pi 'naɾ
pinar,
pine grove

'u nas por pi 'ɲo nes 'o tɾas
Unas por piñones, otras
Some for pine nuts some
por βaj 'laɾ   por βaj 'laɾ   la la la la
por bailar,   por bailar,   la, la, la, la...
for   dancing, for   dancing, la, la, la, la...

baj 'lan do͜ j   paɾ 'tjen do la(s)
Bailando   y   partiendo   las
Dancing   and cracking   the
se 'ra nas   'be ʎas
serranas   bellas
mountain girls beautiful

um pi 'ɲom por 'o tɾo   ðe͜ a 'mor las
un piñón   por otro,   de amor   las
a   pine nut for another of love   the
sa 'e tas
saetas
arrows

Serranas de Cuenca iban al pinar,
unas por piñones, otras por bailar,
por bailar, la, la, la, la...

Bailando y partiendo las serranas
bellas
un piñón por otro, de amor las
saetas
huelgan de trocar:
unas por piñones, otras por bailar,
otras por bailar, por bailar.

Serranas de Cuenca iban al pinar,
unas por piñones, otras por bailar,
por bailar, la, la, la, la...

Entre rama y rama cuando el ciego
dios
pide al sol los ojos por verlas
mejor;
los ojos del sol las veréis pisar:
unas por piñones, otras por bailar,
otras por bailar, por bailar.

———————— • ————————

Mountain girls from Cuenca went
to the pine grove,
Some looking for pine nuts, others
for dancing, for dancing.

'wel ɣan de tɾo 'kaɾ
huelgan de trocar:
they enjoy   exchanging

'u nas por pi 'ɲo nes 'o tɾas
Unas   por piñones,   otras
Some   for   pine nuts   some
por ßaj 'laɾ   por ßaj 'laɾ   la la la la
por bailar,   por bailar,   la, la, la, la ...
for   dancing, for   dancing, la, la, la, la ...

Dancing and cracking one nut and another, the beautiful girls
Enjoy dodging the arrows of love:
Some looking for pine nuts, others for dancing, others for dancing, for dancing.

se 'ra naz   ðe   'kweŋ ka 'i ßan al
Serranas   de   Cuenca   iban   al
Mountain girls from   Cuenca   went   to the
pi 'naɾ
pinar,
pine grove

Mountain girls from Cuenca went to the pine grove,
Some looking for pine nuts, others for dancing, for dancing.

'u nas por pi 'ɲo nes 'o tɾas
Unas   por piñones,   otras
Some   for   pine nuts   some
por ßaj 'laɾ   por ßaj 'laɾ   la la la la
por bailar,   por bailar,   la, la, la, la ...
for   dancing, for   dancing, la, la, la, la ...

Amidst the branches blind Cupid
Asks the Sun's eyes to let him see the girls better;
You can see them scorning the eyes of the sun:
Some looking for pine nuts, others for dancing, others for dancing, for dancing.

'en tɾe 'ra   ma j 'ra ma 'kwan do̯ el
Entre rama   y   rama   cuando   el
In between branch and   branch when   the
'θje ɣo 'ðjos
ciego   dios
blind   god [Cupid]

'pi ðe al 'sol   los 'o xos
pide al sol   los ojos
asks   from the sun the eyes
por 'ßeɾ las   me 'xor
por verlas   mejor;
in order to see them better

los 'o xos del   'sol las be 'ɾejs pi 'saɾ
los ojos del   sol las veréis pisar:
the eyes   of the sun them you'll see tread on

'u nas por pi 'ɲo nes 'o tɾas
Unas por piñones, otras
Some for pine nuts some
por ßaj 'laɾ 'o tɾas por ßaj 'laɾ por ßaj 'laɾ
por bailar, otras por bailar, por bailar.
for dancing, some for dancing, for dancing.

21
'gɾa θja 'mi a
Gracia mía
Grace mine

'gɾa θja 'mi a 'xu ɾo‿a 'ðjos
Gracia mía, juro   a Dios
Grace   mine I swear to God

ke 'sojs   tam 'be ʎa kɾja 'tu ɾa
que sois   tan bella   criatura
that you are such beautiful creature

ˌke‿a peɾ 'ðeɾ se la‿eɾ mo 'su ɾa
que a perderse la hermosura
that if it got lost the beauty

Gracia mía, juro a Dios
que sois tan bella criatura
que a perderse la hermosura
se tiene de hallar su voz.

Fuera bien aventurada
en perderse en vos mi vida
porque viniera perdida
para salir más ganada.

¡Ah! Seréis hermosuras dos
en una sola figura,
que a perderse la hermosura
se tiene de haller en vos.

se   'tje ne ðe͜a 'ʎar su 'βoθ
se   tiene de hallar su voz.
one must   find   its voice

'fwe ɾa 'βje n   a ˌβen tu 'ɾa ða
Fuera bien   aventurada
It would be well happy

em per 'ðeɾ se͜(e)m 'bos mi 'Bi ða
en perderse   en   vos mi vida
in   losing itself in   you my life

ˌpor ke βi 'nje ɾa   per 'ði ða
porque viniera   perdida
because it would come lost

'pa ɾa   sa 'lir ˌmaz   ɣa 'na ða
para   salir más   ganada.
in order to come out more won

'a   se 'ɾejs   er mo 'su ɾas 'dos
¡Ah! Seréis   hermosuras dos
Ah! You will be beauties   two

en 'u na 'so la fi 'ɣu ɾa
en una sola figura
in one   only figure

ˌke͜a per 'ðeɾ se la͜er mo 'su ɾa
que a perderse la hermosura
that if it got lost   the beauty

se   'tje ne ðe͜a 'ʎaɾ em 'bos
se   tiene de hallar en vos.
one must   find [it] in   you

En vuestros verdes ojuelos
nos mostráis vuestro valor
que son causa del amor
y las pestañas son cielos, son cielos;
nacieron por bien de nos.

Gracia mía, juro a Dios
que sois tan bella criatura
que a perderse la hermosura
se tiene de hallar en vos, se tiene de hallar en vos.

———————— • ————————

My gracious one, I swear to God
That you are so beautiful
That if beauty were lost
One could find its voice in you.

I would count myself happy
To lose my life in you
For it would come to you a loser
And come out a winner.

Ah! You are two beauties
In one single body,
For if beauty were lost
One could find it in you.

In your little green eyes
You show us your worth;
They are the cause of our love
And their lashes are the heavens, are the heavens;
They were born for our good.

My gracious one, I swear to God
That you are so beautiful
That if beauty were lost
One could find it in you, one could find it in you.

em 'bwes tɾoz 'βer ðes o 'xwe los
En vuestros   verdes   ojuelos
In   your   green   little eyes

noz   mos 'tɾajs 'bwes tɾo βa 'lor
nos   mostráis   vuestro   valor
to us you show   your   worth

ke   'soŋ 'kaw sa   ðel a 'moɾ
que son causa   del amor
for   they are cause of   love

i   las pes ta ɲas‿son
y   las pestañas   son
and the eyelashes   are
'θje los
cielos, son cielos;
heavens are heavens

na 'θje ɾon   por 'βjen de   'nos
nacieron   por bien de   nos.
they were born for [the] good of us

'gɾa θja 'mi a 'xu ɾo‿a 'ðjos
Gracia mía, juro   a Dios
Grace   mine I swear to God

ke 'sojs   tam 'be ʎa   kɾja 'tu ɾa
que sois   tan bella   criatura
that you are such beautiful creature

ˌke‿a peɾ 'ðeɾ se la‿er mo 'su ɾa
que a perderse   la hermosura
that if it got lost the beauty

se   'tje ne ðe‿a 'ʎaɾ   em 'bos
se   tiene de hallar   en vos.
one must   find [it] in you

IV. *Catalan Songs*

"Elegia eterna" (Eternal Elegy)
"L'ocell profeta" (The Prophet Bird)

Granados wrote music for two Catalan poems. "Elegia eterna" is based on a poem by Apel.les Mestres (1854–1936). The poem first appeared in a collection of Mestres's work entitled *Cants íntims* (Intimate Songs), published in Barcelona in 1889. It is a sweet and langorous poem, rather ingenious in a naive way, very much in the fashion of the fin-de-siècle, in the style known in Barcelona as *modernisme*, akin to the convoluted prissiness of *Art Nouveau*.

The second song, "L'ocell profeta," is the work of a woman who has left a rather light mark on the history of Catalan literature: Isabel Maria del Carme Castellví i Gordon, countess of Castellar. This is anything but a popular piece: No folk song would call night "discreet" or use words like *suavitat* ('softness'), *exquisida*, and *infinit*.

22
ə lə ˈʒi ə (ə) ˈtɛr nə
Elegia eterna
Elegy eternal

əɫ	pəpə ˈʎo	no	li ˌa		ˈðit ˈmaj
El	**papalló**	**no**	**li ha**		**dit mai:**
The	butterfly	not	to her has		said never

no	ˈɤozə	rəβə ˈlar li		sum ˈmaɫ
no	**gosa**	**re velar-li**		**son mal;**
not	dares	to reveal to her	his	sorrow

El papalló no li ha dit mai:
no gosa revelar-li son mal;
però glateix d'amor per una rosa
que idolatra a la brisa matinal.

La brisa matinal enamorada
per la boira es desviu
i la boira perduda i afollada,
decandint-se d'amor, adora el riu,
adora el riu.[1]

pə 'ro glə 'tɛʃ   də 'mor par ˌu nə 'rɔ zə
peró glateix   d'amor per una rosa
but   it quivers of love for a   rose

ka‿j ðu 'la trə‿(ə) lə 'βri zə mə ti 'nał
que idolatra   a la brisa matinal.
that adores   the   breeze morning

la   'βri zə mə ti 'nał ə nə mu 'ra ðə
La brisa matinal   enamorada
The breeze morning   in love

pər lə 'βɔj rə‿(ə)z dez 'βiw
per la boira es desviu
with the mist   itself pains

i   la 'βɔj rə pər 'ðu ðə‿j‿ə fu 'ʎa ðə
i   la boira perduda i   afollada,
and the mist   lost   and crazed

də kən 'din sə ðə' ɾor ə 'ðo ɾə‿(ə)ł 'riw
decandint-se d'amor, adora el   riu,
decaying   with love adores   the river,

ə 'ðo ɾə‿(ə)ł 'riw
adora el   riu,
adores   the river,

mez 'aj əł 'riw ən ʒu ʁə 'sat fu 'ʒi ə
Mes, ai!, el riu enjogassat fugia,
But   o! the river playful   fleeted

en ʒu ʁə 'sat də   pə 'ɲał əm pə 'ɲal
enjogassat, de   penyal en penyal.
playful   from boulder to boulder

Mes, ai!, el riu enjogassat fugia,
enjogassat,[2] de penyal en penyal.
La boira enamorada el riu seguia,
i a la boira la brisa matinal.

En tant, vegent-se[3] abandonada i
sola,
s'ha desfullat la flor,
i al damunt d'aquell tronc sense
corol·la
s'atura el papalló, clou l'ala, i mor.
Ah! Clou l'ala i mor, clou l'ala i
mor.[4]

———————— • ————————

The butterfly never told her:
He dares not reveal his torment;
but he quivers with love for a rose
who adores the morning breeze.

The morning breeze, in love
with the mist, is suffering,
and the mist, lost and crazed,
languishing with love, adores the
river, adores the river.

But, oh!, the playful river ran,
playful, from boulder to boulder.
The lovelorn mist followed him,
and the morning breeze followed
the mist.

Meanwhile, seeing herself
abandoned and alone,
the flower lost her petals,
and on top of that stem with no
corolla
the butterfly stops, closes his
wings, and dies.
Ah! He closes his wings and dies,
closes his wings and dies.

la 'βɔj ɾə (ə) nə mu 'ɾa ðə (ə)ɫ 'riw
La boira enamorada   el riu
The mist   in love   the river
sə 'ɣi a
seguiə,
it followed

jə lə 'βɔj ɾə lə 'βɾi zə   mə ti 'naɫ
i a la boira la brisa   matinal.
and the mist   the breeze   morning

ən 'tan   bə 'ʒen sə (ə) βən ðu 'na ðə
En tant,   vegent-se   abandonada
Meanwhile seeing itself abandoned
j   'sɔ lə
i   sola,
and lonely

'sa ðəs fu 'ʎat   lə 'flɔ
s'ha desfullat   la flor,
itself has lost its petals the flower

j   əɫ də 'mun də 'kɛʎ 'trɔŋ ˌsen sə
i   al damunt d'aquell tronc sense
and on top   of that   stem without
ku 'rɔ lə
corol·la
corolla

sə 'tu ɾə＿(ə)ɫ pə pə 'ʎo
s'atura　el　papalló,
stops itself the butterfly
'a　'klɔw 'la lə＿j　'mɔɾ
Ah! clou l'ala　i　mor.
Ah! closes the wing and dies
'klɔw 'la lə＿j　'mɔɾ
clou l'ala　i　mor.
closes the wing and dies

23
lu 'seʎ pɾu 'fɛ tə
L'ocell profeta
The bird prophet

'kan tə＿(ə)w 'seʎ əj 'mat 'kan tə＿(ə)w 'seʎ
Canta, aucell　aimat! Canta, aucell
Sing　bird　beloved Sing　bird
pɾu 'fɛ tə
profeta!
prophet

'laj ɾ(ə) 'es swə βi 'tat i　lə　'nit
L'aire　és suavitat　i　la　nit
The air is　softness　and the night
dis 'kɾe tə 'a
discreta. Ah!
discreet.　O!

'ʒɔ jə ðə mun 'kɔr tə　kən 'sɔ‿'es
Joia de mon cor, ta　cançó és
Joy　of my　heart your song　is
lə　'βi ðə
la　vida.
the life

Canta, aucell aimat!
Canta, aucell profeta!
L'aire és suavitat
i la nit discreta.
Ah! Joia de mon cor,
ta cançó és la vida.
Canta la veu d'or.
Canta, canta ma cançó exquisida.

Ah, gentil aucell,
mestre en poesia.
Diu l'amor novell
quan s'escolaˢ el dia:
Ah! Vola per ma nit
fosca d'enyorança.
Deixa al fons del pit,
deixa, deixa, somnis d'esperança.

'kan tə lə   'βεw 'ðɔr   'kan tə 'kan tə
Canta la veu d'or.   Canta, canta
Sing   the voice of gold   Sing,   sing
mə kan 'so‿əks ki 'zi ðə
ma cançó   exquisida.
my song   exquisite.

'a   ʒən 'til əw 'seʎ 'mεs trə‿(ə)m
Ah, gentil aucell, mestre en
Ah! gentle bird   master   in
pu ə 'zi ə
poesia.
poetry.

'diw lə 'mor nu 'βeʎ 'kwan səs 'kɔ lə
Diu l'amor novell quan s'escola
Says the love new   that   it shortens
(ə)ł 'ði ə 'a
el dia: Ah!
the day: Ah!

'bɔ lə pər mə   'nit 'fos kə
Vola per ma   nit   fosca
Fly   through my night dark
ðə ɲu 'ɾan sə
d'enyorança.
with longing

'de ʃə‿(ə)ł 'fons   dəł 'pit 'de ʃə
Deixa al fons   del   pit, deixa,
Leave in the bottom of the chest leave
'ðe ʃə 'sɔm niz ðəs pə 'ɾan sə
deixa somnis d'esperança.
leave dreams of hope

De l'amor ardit
ma tardor s'omplena;
l'hora d'infinit
nova llum ofrena.
Ah! Porta per l'espai
l'amorosa troba.
Canta, ardent i gai,
canta, canta una aubada nova.

———————— • ————————

Sing, beloved bird!
Sing, prophet bird!
The air is all softness
And the night discreet.
Ah! Joy of my heart,
Your song is my life.
Let your golden voice sing.
Let it, let it sing my exquisite
song.

Ah, gentle bird,
Master in poesy.
The new love says
When the day fades away:
Ah! Fly through my night
Dark with nostalgia.
Leave at the bottom of your heart,
Leave, leave those dreams of hope.

My autumn gets filled
With valiant love;
The infinite hour
Offers a new light.
Ah! Bring through the air
The song of love.
Sing, ardent and gay.
Sing, sing a new dawn song.

dǝ lǝ 'moɾ ǝɾ 'ðit mǝ tǝɾ 'ðo   sum 'plɛ nǝ
De l'amor ardit ma tardor   s'omplena;
Of the love brave my autumn fills itself

'lɔ ɾǝ   ðiɲ fi 'nit 'nɔ βǝ 'ʎum
l'hora   d'infinit   nova llum
the hour of infinite new   light
u 'fɾɛ nǝ 'a
ofrena. Ah!
it offers Ah!

'pɔr tǝ pǝr   lǝs 'paj lǝ mu 'ɾo zǝ
Porta per   l'espai l'amorosa
It transports in the space the amorous
'tɾɔ βǝ
troba.
poem

'kan tǝ‿(ǝ)ɾ 'ðen i   'ɣaj 'kan tǝ 'kan tǝ
Canta, ardent i   gai, canta, canta
Sing   ardent and gay sing   sing
u nǝ‿(ǝ)w 'βa ðǝ 'nɔ βǝ
una aubada   nova.
a   aubade   new.

——Chapter V

Songs of Falla

I. *Siete canciones populares*

(Seven Popular Songs)

"El Paño Moruno" (The Moorish Cloth)
"Seguidilla Murciana" (Seguidilla from Murcia)
"Asturiana" (Asturian)
"Jota" (Jota)
"Nana" (Lullaby)
"Canción" (Song)
"Polo" (Polo)

Falla's *Siete Canciones populares* represent not only a discovery of the possibilities of Spanish folk tunes for concert recital, but also a brief compendium of motifs and techniques from Spanish folklore. Some general characteristics worth noting become apparent in this brief cycle. The main one may be the extremely connotative character of the Spanish folk lyric. We observe this both in the very free and associative use of metaphor (Moorish cloth, a glass roof, a coin all stand for something left unnamed) and in the blatant incoherence of some songs. The popular technique at the root of this incoherence is that of *coplas*. The word is obviously related to 'couplets', but it has come to mean any series of short verses held together by a common rhythm or melody (so they can be sung to the same tune in whatever order the memory of the singer brings them to mind). A given set of *coplas* will also share, beyond the signification of the verses, beyond any narrative plot, a colorful system of metaphors. *Coplas* are a kind of poetic sharpshooting rather than a concerted offensive. Even though these seven pieces have been gathered from distinct and separate regions of Spain, they all share a certain mood, a certain nature; they are all, in a way, *coplas*.

"El paño Moruno" surely refers to the complex honor code of southern Spain. The cloth in question may be a metaphor for one's reputation; it may also stand for the woman who does not guard her chastity. The answer, as in most of these pieces, is not to be found within the song; indeed ambiguity may be one of the effects sought and one of the composition's virtues.

Seguidilla is the generic name for one of the flamenco dances; this particular one originated, the title informs us, in the region of Murcia, to the east of Andalusia. The middle "stanza" makes allusion to the muleteers who developed it to entertain each other during their travels. The *copla* style is clearest here; the first and third stanzas share little beyond a practical morality: Do not accuse others of your own defects; promiscuity is dangerous. We sense here, as in "El paño moruno," in the reference in both songs to economic value and depreciation, an expression of the reification of society, and of women in particular.

The "Asturiana," from the distant and verdant northern region of Asturias, shows a disarming simplicity, a simplicity fraught with unconscious signification. The green pine is a symbol of sexual desire as old as Spanish literature itself. Its tears may be nothing more than drops of rain on its needles, which a pathetic fallacy equates to the weeping of the singer.

The "Jota" is the typical dance of Aragon. As in most of Spain's folk lyrics, the love scene centers on the first-floor window through which the lovers speak to each other. Also typical is the presence of the mother, severe here, sympathetic in other compositions of this anthology.

The "Nana" or lullaby, and the "Canción" need little explanation beyond what we have said, except that the "Canción" mysteriously echoes a few incomplete words from another song, a song that not surprisingly involves the mother of the young woman in love.

Finally, the "Polo" takes us back to Andalusia and to flamenco. *Polo* is one of the song forms (with no instrumental accompaniment) in the oldest, most pure flamenco, the *cante jondo*, 'deep song'. In compositions such as this, the meaningful dimension of language—always secondary in Spanish folk poetry—reaches its minimal expression. Most of the song is taken by the exclamation "ay", elongated here beyond its usual one syllable: it is pronounced exceptionally *a-i*. The rest of the lyrics provide a few color notes of significance as if to illustrate that the lovesickness of the singer has reached a climax of pain beyond all coherence, beyond grammar.

24
el 'pa ɲo mo 'ɾu no
El paño Moruno
The cloth Moorish

,al   'pa ɲo 'fi no‿en la
Al   paño fino en la
To the cloth fine in the
'tjen da, al   'pa ɲo 'fi no‿en la 'tjen da,
tienda, al   paño fino en la tienda
shop, to the cloth fine in the shop,

u na 'maɲ tʃa ˌle
Una mancha le
A   stain   to it
ka 'jo, u na 'maɲ tʃa ˌle cayó
cayó, una mancha le cayó;
it fell, a   stain   to it it fell

por 'me nos 'pɾe θjo se
Por menos precio se
For less   price   itself
'βen de, por 'me nos 'pɾe θjo se   vende
vende, por menos precio se   vende,
sells,   for less   price   itself sells

'por ke peɾ 'ðjo su
porque perdió su
because it lost   its
βa 'loɾ, 'por ke peɾ 'ðjo su valor
valor, porque perdió su valor.
value, because it lost   its value

Al paño fino en la tienda, al paño
fino en la tienda
una mancha le cayó, una mancha le
cayó;
por menos precio se vende, por
menos precio se vende,
porque perdió su valor, porque
perdió su valor.

———————— • ————————

On the fine cloth in the store, on
the fine cloth in the store
fell a stain, fell a stain;
Now it sells for less money, now it
sells for less money,
for it lost its value, for it lost its
value.

25
se ɣi 'ði ʎa muɾ 'θja na
Seguidilla Murciana
Seguidilla from Murcia

kwal 'kje ɾa ˌkel   te 'xa ðo 'teŋ ga ðe
Cualquiera que el tejado tenga de
Anyone   who the roof   has   of
'βi ðɾjo 'teŋga ðe 'βi ðɾjo
vidrio, tenga de vidrio,
glass, has of glass

ˌno 'ðe βe ti 'ɾar 'pje ðɾas
no debe tirar piedras
not should throw stones
al ˌdel   βe 'θi no
al del   vecino.
to one of the neighbor.

a r 'je ɾo(s) 'se mos 'pwe ðe ken
Arrieros   semos; puede que en
Muleteers   we are it's possible that on
el ka 'mi no nos   en kon 'tɾe mos
el camino nos   encontremos.
the road   each other we meet.

ˌPor tu   'mu tʃa ˌin kons 'tan ˌθja ˌjo
Por tu   mucha inconstancia   yo
For your great inconstancy   I
te kom 'pa ɾo jo te kom 'pa ɾo
te comparo, yo te comparo
you compare, I you compare

Cualquiera que el tejado tenga de
vidrio, tenga de vidrio,
no debe tirar piedras al del vecino.

Arrieros semos; puede que en el
camino
nos encontremos.

Por tu mucha inconstancia
yo te comparo, yo te comparo
con peseta que corre
de mano en mano,
que al fin se borra,
y creyéndola falsa
nadie la toma, nadie la toma.

— • —

Anyone whose roof is made of
glass, is made of glass
Should not throw stones
To his neighbor's.

We're muleteers!
Perhaps we shall meet
On the road.

Because of your great inconstancy
I compare you
To a coin that goes
From hand to hand;
It finally fades
And, thinking it false,
Nobody takes it.

‚kom pe 'se ta ke   'ko re de
con   peseta   que corre   de
with peseta   that runs   from

'ma no‿em 'ma no
mano   en mano,
hand   in hand,

k(e)‿al   'fin se   'βo ra i
que al   fin se   borra, y
that to the end itself erases and

kɾe 'jen do la 'fal sa
creyéndola   falsa
thinking it   false

'na ðje la 'to ma, 'na ðje la 'to ma
nadie la toma, nadie   la toma.
no one it takes, no one   it takes

26
as tu 'rja na
Asturiana
Asturian

‚por 'βer   si me kon so 'la βa
Por ver   si me consolaba
For seeing if me it consoled

a ri 'me m(e)   a‿um 'pi no   'βer ðe
Arriméme   a un pino   verde
Approached myself to a   pine tree green

‚por 'βer   si me kon so 'la βa
Por ver   si me consolaba
For seeing if me it consoled

Por ver si me consolaba
arriméme a un pino verde,
por ver si me consolaba.
Por verme llorar, lloraba
y el pino, como era verde,
por verme llorar lloraba.

,por 'βer me   ʎo 'rar ʎo 'ra βa
Por verme   llorar, lloraba
For seeing me cry   it cried

i   el 'pi no   'ko mo e ra   'βer ðe
y el pino,   como era   verde,
and the pine tree as   it was green

,por 'βer me   ʎo 'rar ʎo 'ra βa
Por verme   llorar, lloraba
For seeing me cry   it cried

To see if it would comfort me
I leaned against a green pine tree,
To see if it would comfort me.
On seeing me cry, it cried,
The pine tree, being green,
On seeing me cry, it cried.

27
'xota
Jota
Jota

'di θeŋ ke ,no ,nos   ke 're mos
Dicen   que no nos   queremos
They say that not each other we love

'por ke ,no ,noz 'ben   a 'βlar
porque no nos ven   hablar;
because not us   they see speak

a tu ,ko ra 'θon j__al   'mi o
a tu   corazón   y al   mío
to your heart   and to the mine

se lo 'pwe ðen pre ɣun'tar
se lo pueden   preguntar.
to it they can   ask.

Dicen que no nos queremos
porque no nos ven hablar;
a tu corazón y al mío
se lo pueden preguntar.
Dicen que no nos queremos
porque no nos ven hablar.
  Ya me despido de ti,
  ya me despido de ti,
  de tu casa y tu ventana,
  y aunque no quiera tu madre,
  adiós, niña, hasta mañana,
  adiós, niña, hasta mañana.
  Ya me despido de ti,
  aunque no quiera tu madre.

———————— • ————————

'di θeŋ   ke   ˌno ˌnos   ke 're mos
Dicen   que no nos   queremos
They say that not each other we love

'por ke ˌno ˌnoz 'ben   a 'βlaɾ
porque no nos ven   hablar.
because not us   they see speak

ˌʝa   me   ðes 'pi ðo   ðe   'ti
ya   me   despido   de   ti,
Now myself I take leave from you

ˌʝa   me   ðes 'pi ðo   ðe   'ti
ya   me   despido   de   ti,
Now myself I take leave from you

de   tu   'ka sa i   tu   βen 'ta na
de   tu   casa y   tu   ventana,
From your house and your window

ʝ   'awŋ ke   no 'kje ɾa   tu   'ma ðɾe
y   aunque   no quiera   tu   madre
And even though not she wants your mother

a' ðjos   ni ɲ(a) 'as ta ma 'ɲa na
Adiós,   niña,   hasta mañana.
Goodbye child   until tomorrow.

a' ðjos   ni ɲ(a) 'as ta ma 'ɲa na
Adiós,   niña,   hasta mañana.
Goodbye child   until tomorrow.

ˌʝa   me   ðes 'pi ðo   ðe   'ti
Ya   me   despido   de   ti,
Now myself I take leave from you

They say we don't love one
another
because they don't see us speak;
your heart and mine
should be asked about that.
They say we don't love one
another
because they don't see us speak.
   Now I take leave from you,
   Now I take leave from you,
   From your house and from your
   window,
   And even though your mother
   doesn't like it,
   Goodbye, my girl, 'til
   tomorrow.
   Goodbye, my girl, 'til
   tomorrow.
   Now I take leave from you,
   Even though your mother
   doesn't like it.

ɟ　　'awŋ ke　　no 'kje ɾa　　tu　　'ma ðɾe
Y　　aunque　　no quiera　　tu　　madre
And even though not she wants your mother

28
'na na
Nana
Lullaby

'dwer me te 'ni ɲo 'dwer me
Duérmete, niño, duerme,
Sleep　　　　child　sleep

'dwer me mi‿'al ma
duerme, mi alma.
Sleep　　my soul

'dwer me te ˌlu θe 'ri to de la　ma 'na na
Duérmete, lucerito　de la mañana.
Sleep　　　　little star　　of the morning

na 'ni ta　　　'na na
Nanita,　　　nana.
Little lullaby, lullaby

na 'ni ta　　　'na na
nanita,　　　nana,
Little lullaby, lullaby

'dwer me te ˌlu θe 'ri to de la　ma 'na na
Duérmete, lucerito　de la mañana.
Sleep　　　　little star　　of the morning

Duérmete, niño, duerme,
duerme, mi alma,
duérmete lucerito
de la mañana.
Nanita, nana, nanita, nana.
Duérmete lucerito de la mañana.

———————— • ————————

Sleep, my child, sleep,
Sleep, my darling,
Sleep, little star
Of morning.
Lullaby, lullaby.
Sleep, little star
Of morning.

29
kan 'θjon
Canción
Song

'por traj 'ðo ɾes ˌtus 'o xos
Por traidores, tus ojos,
For treacherous your eyes,

boj a _____ (e)n te 'rar los
voy a   enterrarlos.
I am going to bury them.

ˌno 'sa βes   lo   ke   'kwes ta
No sabes   lo   que cuesta,
Not you know (the) what it costs

del   'aj ɾe ni ɲa el   mi 'rar los
"del   aire," niña, el   mirarlos.
from the air   child (the) to look at them.

'ma ðɾe a ˌla o 'ri ʎa
"Madre a la orilla."
Mother to the shore.

ni ɲa el   mi 'rar los
Niña, el   mirarlos.
child (the) to look at them.

'di θen   ke   'no me 'kje ɾes
Dicen   que no me quieres,
They say that not me you love

Por traidores, tus ojos,
Voy a enterrarlos.
No sabes lo que cuesta,
"del aire," niña, el mirarlos.
"Madre a la orilla."
Niña, el mirarlos.
  Dicen que no me quieres,
  Ya me has querido.
  Váyase lo ganado,
  "del aire," por lo perdido.
  "Madre a la orilla."
Por lo perdido.

———————————— • ————————————

Because your eyes are traitors,
I am going to bury them.
You don't know how hard it is,
"from the air," my love, to look at
them.
"Mother, to the shore."
My love, to look at them.
  They say you don't love me,
  You loved me before.
  Let go what was won,
  "From the air," for what is
  now lost.
  "Mother, to the shore."
  For what is now lost.

ʝa   m(e̯) 'as   ke 'ɾi ðo
ya   me   has   querido.
Already me   you have loved.

'baʝ a se lo ɣa 'na ðo del   'aj ɾe
Váyase lo ganado, "del   aire,"
Let it go the won   from the air
por lo per ði ðo
por lo perdido.
for the lost.

'ma ðɾe̯ a ˌla̯ o 'ɾiha
"Madre a la orilla."
Mother to the shore.

por lo per 'ðiðo
Por lo perdido.
For the lost

30
'po lo
Polo
Polo

'a 'i 'gwar ðo̯ 'u na 'aj
¡Ay!, guardo una, ¡ay!,
Ah I keep   a   ah

'gwar ðo̯ u na 'pe na̯ em̱ mi pe tʃo 'a 'i
guardo una pena en mi pecho, ¡ay!
I keep   a   sorrow in my chest, ah!

ˌke a 'na ðʝe ˌse   la ði 'ɾe
que a nadie se   la diré.
that to nobody to them it I will tell.

¡Ay!
Guardo una, ¡ay!,
guardo una pena en mi pecho,
¡ay!,
que a nadie se la diré.
Malhaya el amor, malhaya,
¡ay!
y quien me lo dio a entender.
¡Ay!

——— • ———

ma 'la ʝa‿el   a mor ma 'la ʝa 'a 'i
Malhaya el   amor, malhaya, ¡ay!
Cursed be (the) love,   cursed be, ah!

i   'kjem   me   lo 'djo‿a
y   quien   me   lo dio a
and s/he who to me it gave to
(e)n ten 'deɾ 'a 'i
entender.   ¡Ay!
understand,   Ah!

Ah!
I keep, ah!,
I keep a sorrow in my heart,
ah!,
And I'll tell no one!
Love be cursed, be cursed!
ah,
And the one who taught it to me,
Ah!

II. *Tus ojillos negros*

(*Your Black Eyes*)

"Tus ojillos negros" (Your Black Eyes)

Falla gave this song the subtitle *canción andaluza* and based it on a poem by the Andalusian writer and journalist Cristóbal de Castro (Córdoba, 1880). It is a typical love song devoted to the eyes of a young woman. There are no surprises in this piece; it is a repository of themes and *topoi* from popular poetry. The song was dedicated to the Marquis and Marchioness of Alta Villa.

31
tus o 'xi ʎos 'ne ɣros
Tus ojillos negros
Your little eyes black

'ɟo no 'se   'ke   'tje nen tus
Yo no sé   qué   tienen tus
I   not know what have   your

o 'xi ʎos 'ne ɣros
ojillos   negros
little eyes black

ke me 'ðan pe 'sa ɾes   i   me
que me dan pesares   y   me
that me they give sorrow and me it

'ɣus ta   'βer los
gusta   verlos,
pleases to see them.

Yo no sé qué tienen tus ojillos negros
que me dan pesares y me gusta verlos,
que me dan pesares y me gusta verlos.
Son tan juguetones y tan zalameros,
sus miradas prontas llegan tan adentro,
que hay quien asegura que Dios los ha hecho
como para muestra de lo que es lo bueno,
de lo que es la gloria, de lo que es el cielo.

ke   me   'ðan pe 'sa ɾes   i   me
que me dan pesares   y   me
that me they give sorrow and me it
'ɣus ta   'βer los
gusta   verlos.
pleases to see them.

'son taŋ   xu ɣe 'to nes i   tan
Son tan   juguetones y   tan
They are so playful   and so
θa la 'me ɾos
zalameros,
graceful

suz mi 'ɾa ðas 'pɾon tas 'ʎe ɣan tan
sus mirades   prontas llegan tan
their looks   quick   arrive   so
a 'ðen tɾo
adentro,
inwards

ke 'aj   kjen   a se 'ɣu ɾa ke
que hay   quien asegura   que
that there are people who swear that
'ðjos los   a   'e tʃo
Dios los   ha hecho
God   them has made

'ko mo pa ɾa 'mwes tɾa ðe lo   k(e)' es
como   para muestra de lo que   es
as   for   example of that which is
lo 'βwe no
lo bueno,
the good

Mas, por otra parte, ¡son tan embusteros!
Dicen tantas cosas que desdicen luego,
que hay quien asegura que Dios los ha hecho
como para muestra de lo que es tormento,
de lo que es desdicha, de lo que es infierno.

Y es que hay en tus ojos como hay en los cielos,
noches muy obscuras, días muy serenos.
Y hay en tus miradas maridaje eterno
de amorcillos locos y desdenes cuerdos,
y entre sus penumbras y sus centelleos
brillantes afanes y tus pensamientos,
como entre las sombras de la noche obscura
brillan los relámpagos con su vivo fuego.

de lo   k(e) 'es   la   'ɣlo ɾja ðe lo
de lo   que es   la gloria, de lo
of that which is the glory   of that

k(e)' es   el   'θje lo
que   es el   cielo.
which is   the heaven

,mas por 'o tɾa   'par te 'son
Mas, por otra   parte, ¡son
But   on the other part   they are

tan em bus 'te ɾos
tan   embusteros!
so   deceitful

'di θen   tan tas 'ko sas ke
Dicen   tantas   cosas   que
They say so many things   that they

ðez 'ði θen 'lwe ɣo
desdicen   luego,
deny   later

ke 'aj   kjen   a se 'ɣu ɾa ke
que hay   quien asegura   que
that there are people who swear that

'ðjos los   a   'e tʃo
Dios los   ha hecho
God   them has made

'ko mo pa ɾa 'mwes tɾa ðe lo   k(e) 'es
como   para muestra de lo   que   es
as   for   example of that which is

tor 'men to
tormento,
torment

Luces que parece que se están muriendo
y que de improviso resucitan luego,
y que de improviso resucitan luego.
Sombras adorables, llenas de misterio
como tus amores, como mis deseos.
Algo que da vida, mucho que da miedo.
Yo no sé qué tienen tus ojillos negros
que me dan pesares y ¡me gusta verlos!

——————————— • ———————————

I don't know what your black eyes have:
They make me sad, but I like to see them,
They make me sad, but I like to see them.
They are so playful and so graceful
Their quick glances reach so deep inside me
That one may well say that God made those eyes
As an example of what good is,
What glory is, what the heavens are.

Yet, on the other hand, they are so deceitful!
They say so many things only to deny them later,
That one may well say that God made them
As an example of what torment is,
What unhappiness is, what hell is.

de lo   k(e)   'es dez 'ði t∫a   ðe lo
de lo   que   es desdicha,   de lo
of that which is   unhappiness of that
k(e)   'es im 'fjer no
que   es infierno.
which is   hell

j   'es ke   'aj   en   tus   'o xos
Y   es   que hay   en   tus   ojos
And it is that there is in your eyes
ko mo   'aj   en los   'θje los
como   hay   en los cielos,
as   there is in the sky

'no t∫es muj os 'ku ɾas 'di as muj se 'ɾe nos
noches   muy obscuras, días   muy serenos.
nights   very dark   days   very serene

j   'aj   en   tuz   mi 'ɾa ðaz ma ɾi 'ða xe
Y   hay   en   tus   miradas   maridaje
and there is in your gazes   marriage
(e) 'teɾ no
eterno
eternal

de̯ a mor 'θi ʎos 'lo kos i   ðez 'ðe nes
de amorcillos   locos   y   desdenes
of little loves   crazy   and disdains
'kwer ðos
cuerdos,
sane

In your eyes, as in the sky, there are
Very dark nights, very clear days.
And they show a constant mixture
Of foolish love and wise disdain,
And in their shadows and their sparkles
There are brilliant longings and all your thoughts.
Just as in the shadows of the darkest night
There is the brilliance of lightning with its living fire.

Lights that seem to be dying
And then all of a sudden come back to life,
And then all of a sudden come back to life.
Adorable shadows, full of mystery
Like your love, like my desire.
Something that inspires life, much that frightens.
I don't know what your black eyes have:
They make me sad but I like to see them.

j   'en tɾe   sus   pe 'num bɾas i   sus
y   entre   sus   penumbras   y   sus
and amongst their shadows   and their
θen te 'ʎe os
centelleos
sparkles

bɾi 'ʎan tes a 'fa nes i   tus
brillantes   afanes   y   tus
brilliant   longings and your
pen sa 'mjen tos
pensamientos,
thoughts

'ko mo en tɾe   la(s) 'som bɾas de la
como   entre   las   sombras   de la
as   amongst the   shadows   of the
'no tʃe os 'ku ɾa
noche   obscura
night   dark

'bɾi ʎan   lo(s) re 'lam pa ɣos ‚kon su
brillan   los   relámpagos   con su
they shine the   lightnings   with their
'βi βo 'fwe ɣo
vivo   fuego.
living fire

'lu θes ke   pa 're θe ke   s(e) es 'tam
Luces que parece   que se   están
lights that it seems that they are
mu 'ɾjen do
muriendo
dying

i   ke ðe̯ iɱ pɾo 'βi so re su 'θi tan
y que de improviso   resucitan
and that of a sudden   they resurrect
'lwe ɤo
luego,
later

i   ke ðe̯ iɱ pɾo 'βi so re su 'θi tan
y que de improviso   resucitan
and that of a sudden   they resurrect
'lwe ɤo
luego.
later

'som bɾas a ðo 'ɾa βles 'ʎe naz ðe mis 'te ɾjo
Sombras adorables, llenas de misterio
Shadows adorable   full   of mystery

'ko mo tus a 'mo ɾes 'ko mo miz ðe 'se os
como tus amores, como mis deseos.
like   your loves   like   my desires

'al ɤo   ke ˌða 'βi ða 'mu tʃo
Algo   que da vida, mucho
Something that gives life   much
ke ˌða 'mje ðo
que da miedo.
that gives fear

'ʝo no 'se 'ke 'tje nen tus
Yo no sé   qué tienen tus
I   not know what have   your
o 'xi ʎos 'ne ɤɾos
ojillos negros
little eyes black

ke me 'ðan   pe 'sa ɾes i   me
que me dan   pesares y   ¡me
that me they give sorrow   and me

'ɣus ta   'βer los
gusta   verlos!
it pleases to see them

III. *Obras desconocidas*

(*Unknown Works*)

"Preludios" (Preludes)
"Olas gigantes" (Gigantic Waves)
"Dios mio, que solos se quedan los muertos!" (My God, How Lonely Are the Dead!)
"Oración de las madres que tienen a sus hijos en brazos" (Prayer of the Mothers Holding Their Sons in their Arms)
"Canción andaluza: el pan de ronda" (Andalusian Song: The Bread from Ronda)

These five works for voice and piano were published in 1980 by Unión Musical Española and were given their circumstantial title by the musicologist Enrique Franco. They do not really form a cycle; they are early works of Falla, composed between 1899 and 1915, and show a certain diversity of style. "Preludios" may indeed be Falla's first composition, based on a strangely devout poem by the Basque poet Antonio de Trueba (1819–1899); it refers to the typical Spanish courtship that takes place through the grillwork on a first-floor window. The two songs that follow are based upon poems by Spain's celebrated late Romantic poet Gustavo Adolfo Bécquer (d. 1870) and are characteristic of his violently descriptive style. The last two works are the fruit of Falla's collaboration with María and Gregorio Martínez Sierra (1881–1947, for Gregorio). The "Andalusian song" "El pan de Ronda" was inspired by the enjoyment of a loaf of bread along the streets of the old town of Ronda (in the province of Málaga), a delicacy that apparently prompted María to write a few verses in the popular style of *coplas*, or variations on a motif. Gregorio and María, incidentally, collaborated on many of the works, but they are all published under his name.

32
pɾe 'lu ðjos
Preludios
Preludes

'ma ðɾe 'to ðas las 'no tʃes ˌxun to̯ a
Madre, todas las noches junto a
Mother, all   the nights next   to

miz 're xas
mis rejas
my grills

'kan ta̯ u̯ŋ 'xo βen   ʎo 'ran do̯
canta un joven llorando
sings a   young man crying

in di fe 'ɾen θja
indiferencia:
indifference

'kje ɾe me   'ni ɲa j̯ al   'pje ðe los
"Quiéreme, niña, y al   pie de los
Love me   girl   and at the foot of the

al 'ta ɾes se 'ɾas   ben 'di ta
altares serás   bendita."
altars   you will be blessed

'kje ɾe me   'ni ɲa j̯ al   'pje ðe los
"Quiéreme, niña, y al   pie de los
Love me   girl   and at the foot of the

al 'ta ɾes se 'ɾas   ben 'di ta
altares serás   bendita."
altars   you will be blessed

ˌes ta 'ðul θe to 'na ða tal   po 'ðer 'tje ne
Esta dulce tonada tal poder tiene
This sweet melody such power it has

Madre, todas las noches junto a
mis rejas
canta un joven llorando
indiferencia:
"Quiéreme, niña, y al pie de los
altares séras bendita.
Quiéreme, niña, y al pié de los
altares serás bendita."

Esta dulce tonada tal poder tiene
que me pone al oirla triste y
alegre;
di por qué causa entristecen y
alegran estas tonadas.
Di por qué causa entristecen y
alegran estas tonadas.

"Hija, lo que las niñas como tú
sienten
cuando junto a sus rejas a cantar
vienen
es el preludio del poema más
grande que hay en el mundo.

Tornada en Santa Madre la Virgen
pura
tristezas y alegrías en elle turnan,
y este poema es, niña, el que ha
empezado junto a tus rejas.
Y este poema es, niña, el que ha
empezado junto a tus rejas."

ke   me   'po ne al   o 'ir la   'tris te
que me pone al   oirla   triste
that me it makes when hearing it sad

j   a 'le ɣre
y   alegre;
and happy

'di por 'ke   'kaw sa en tris 'te θen
Di por qué causa   entristecen
tell by what cause   they sadden

j   a 'le ɣran 'es tas to 'na ðas
y   alegran   estas tonadas.
and gladden   these   melodies

'di por 'ke   'kaw sa en tris 'te θen
di por qué causa   entristecen
tell by what cause   they sadden

j   a 'le ɣran 'es tas to 'na ðas
y   alegran   estas tonadas.
and gladden   these   melodies

'i xa   lo   ke   las 'ni ɲas ‚ko mo
"Hija,   lo   que   las niñas como
Daughter that which the girls   like

'tu 'sjen ten
tú sienten
you feel

‚kwan do 'xun to a suz 're xas a
cuando   junto a sus rejas a
when   next   to their grills to

kan 'tar 'βje nen
cantar vienen
sing   they come

Mother, every night at my window
I hear a young man sing,
complaining of my indifference:
"Love me, girl, and by the altar
You will be blessed.
Love me, girl, and by the altar
You will be blessed."

This sweet melody has such power
That when I hear it I become sad
and happy;
Tell me why such melodies
Make people sad and happy.
Tell me why such melodies
Make people sad and happy.

"My daughter, what girls like you
feel
When someone comes to their
windows to sing
Is but the prelude of the greatest
poem
The world will hear.

Once the pure Virgin became the
Holy Mother,
She began feeling sadness and joy,
And this poem is, my girl, the one
that has started
At your window.
And this poem is, my girl, the one
that has started
at your window."

'es el pɾe 'lu ðjo ðel po 'e ma 'maz
es el preludio del poema más
it is the prelude of the poem more

ɣɾan de ke‿'aj en el 'mun do
grande que hay en el mundo.
great that there is in the world

tor 'na ða‿en 'san ta 'ma ðɾe la
Tornada en Santa Madre la
Converted into Holy Mother the

'βir xen 'pu ɾa
Virgen puɾa
Virgin pure

tɾis 'te θas j a le 'ɣɾi as en 'e ʎa
tristezas y alegrías en ella
sadnesses and joys in her

'tur nan
turnan,
take turns

j 'es te po 'e ma‿'es 'ni ɲa‿el ke 'a‿
y este poema es, niña, el que ha
and this poem it is, girl, the one that has

em pe 'θa ðo 'xun to‿a tuz 're xas
empezado junto a tus rejas."
begun next to your grills

j 'es te po 'e ma‿'es 'ni ɲa el ke‿'a
y este poema es, niña, el que ha
and this poem it is, girl, the one that has

em pe 'θa ðo 'xun to‿a tuz 're xas
empezado junta a tus rejas."
begun next to your grills

33
'o las xi 'ɣan tes
Olas gigantes
Waves giant

'o las xi 'ɣan tes ke͜os
Olas gigantes   que os
Waves giant   that yourselves

roŋ 'pejz bra 'man do
rompéis bramando
break   clamoring

en las 'pla jaz de 'sjer tas i   re 'mo tas
en las playas desiertas   y   remotas,
on the beaches desert   and remote

em 'bwel to͜en tre   la(s) 'sa βa naz
envuelto   entre   las   sábanas
wrapped up between the   sheets

d(e)͜es 'pu ma
de   espuma
of   foam

ʎe 'βað me kom bo 'so tras
¡llevadme con vosotras!
take me   with you

'ra fa ɣaz de͜u ra 'kan ke͜a re βa 'tajs
Ráfagas   de huracán, que arrebatáis
Crests   of hurricane that snatch

del   'al to 'βos ke laz mar 'tʃi tas 'o xas
del   alto bosque las marchitas hojas,
of the high forest   the withered   leaves

Olas gigantes que os rompéis
bramando
en las playas desiertas y remotas,
envuelto entre las sábanas de
espuma,
¡llevadme con vosotras!

Ráfagas de huracán, que arrebatáis
del alto bosque las marchitas hojas,
arrastrando en el ciego torbellino,
¡llevadme con vosotras!

Nubes de tempestad que rompe el
rayo
y en fuego ornáis las desprendidas
orlas,
arrebatado entre la niebla oscura,
¡llevadme con vosotras!

¡Llevadme, por piedad![6]
Llevadme, por piedad, adonde el
vértigo
con la razón me arranque la
memoria.
¡Por piedad! ¡Por piedad![7]
¡Tengo miedo de quedarme
con mi dolor a solas,
con mi dolor a solas![8]

———————— • ————————

a ras 'tran do‿en   el   'θje ɤo
arrastrando en   el ciego
dragging   through the blind
tor ße 'ʎi no
torbellino,
turbulence

ʎe 'ßað me kom bo 'so tras
¡llevadme con vosotras!
take me   with you

'nu ßez de teŋ pes 'tað ke   'roŋ pe‿
Nubes de tempestad   que rompe
Clouds of storm   that breaks
(e)l 'ra jo
el   rayo
the lightning

j‿eŋ 'fwe ɤo‿or 'najs laz
y en fuego ornáis   las
and in fire   you adorn the
des pren 'di ðas 'or las
desprendidas   orlas,
loose   borders

a re ßa 'ta ðo‿en tre la 'nje ßla‿os ku ɾa
arrebatado   entre la niebla oscura,
swept away   among the fog   dark

ʎe 'ßað me kom bo 'so tras
¡llevadme con vosotras!
take me   with you

Gigantic waves that break out in a clamor
on deserted and distant beaches,
shroud me with your sheets of foam
and take me with you!

Wind crests of the hurricane, when you tear away
the dead leaves of forests,
dragging everything along in your blind turbulence,
take me with you!

Storm clouds, broken by lightning,
with your borders outlined in fire,
sweep me away in the center of your dark fog,
and take me with you!

Take me, for pity's sake!
Take me, for pity's sake, where the vertigo
would eradicate my memory and my reason.
For pity's sake! For pity's sake!
I am terribly afraid to be left alone with my pain,
alone with my pain!

ʎe 'βað me por pje 'ðað
¡Llevadme, por piedad!
Take me   by   pity

ʎe 'βað me por pje 'ðað a 'ðon de (e)
Llevadme, por piedad, adonde   el
Take me   by pity   where   the
'ber ti ɣo
vértigo
vertigo

kon la ra 'θom me‿a 'raŋ ke   la
con la razón me   arranque la
with the reason me   it pulls out the
me 'mo ɾja
memoria.
memory

por pje ðað   por pje ðað
¡Por piedad! ¡Por piedad!
By pity   By pity

'teŋ go 'mje ðo ðe ke 'ðar me
¡Tengo miedo de quedarme
I have   fear   of remaining

ˌkom mi ðo 'loɾ a 'so las
con   mi dolor a solas,
with my pain   in loneliness

ˌkom mi ðo 'loɾ a 'so las
con   mi dolor a solas!
with my pain   in loneliness

34
'djos 'mi o 'ke 'so los se 'ke ðan loz 'mwer tos
¡Dios mio, que solos se quedan los muertos!
God my how lonely remain the dead

θe 'ra ɾon   sus 'o xos k(e) 'awn
Cerraron   sus ojos   que aún
They closed his eyes   that still

te 'ni a (a) 'βjer tos
tenía abiertos;
he had open

ta 'pa ɾon   su 'ka ɾa kon um 'blaŋ ko
taparon   su cara   con un blanco
they covered his face   with a   white

'ljen θo
lienzo;
cloth

j͜u nos so ʎo 'θan do 'o tros en si 'len θjo
y   unos sollozando   otros   en silencio,
and some weeping   others in silence

de la 'tris te͜ al 'ko βa 'to ðos se
de la triste alcoba   todos se
from the sad   bedroom all

sa 'lje ɾon
salieron.
left

Cerraron sus ojos
que aún tenía abiertos;
taparon su cara
con un blanco lienzo;
y unos sollozando,
otros en silencio,
de la triste alcoba
todos se salieron.

La luz, que en un vaso
ardía en el suelo,
al muro arrojaba
la sombra del lecho,
y entre aquella sombra
veíase a intervalos
dibujarse rígida
la forma del cuerpo.

Despertaba el día
y a su albor primero,
con sus mil ruidos
despertaba el pueblo.
Ante aquel contraste
de vida y misterios,
de luz y tinieblas,
yo pensé un momento:
¡Dios mío, qué solos
se quedan los muertos!⁹

la 'luθ ke (e)n um 'ba so aɾ 'ði a e̯n
La luz, que en un vaso ardía en
the light that on a   vase burned on
el 'swe lo
el suelo,
the floor

al   'mu ɾo a̯ ro 'xa βa la 'som bɾa ðel
al   muro arrojaba   la sombra del
on the wall   it threw   the shadow of the
'le t∫o
lecho,
bed

j 'en tɾe a̯ 'ke ʎa 'som bɾa
y entre   aquella sombra
and amongst that   shadow
be 'i a se a̯ in ter 'βa los
veíase   a   intervalos
one could see with intervals

di βu 'xar se 'ri xi ða la 'for ma
dibujarse rígida la forma
outline itself rigid   the form
ðel   'kwer po
del   cuerpo.
of the corpse

des per 'ta βa e̯l 'di a j a̯ su̯
Despertaba el día y a su
Awakened   the day and to its
al 'βor pɾi 'me ɾo
albor primero,
clarity first

They closed his eyes
that were still open;
they covered his face
with a white cloth;
some people weeping,
others in silence,
they all left
the sad bedroom.

The light, burning
in a vase on the floor,
projected the shadow
of the bed on the wall,
and along with that shadow
one could see at times
the rigid outline
of the dead man's body.

The day was awakening
and with its first light,
with a thousand noises
the village was rising.
Faced with that contrast
of life and mystery,
of light and darkness,
I thought for a moment:
My God, how lonely
are the dead!

kon suz 'mil   ru 'i ðos des per 'ta ßa‿
con sus mil   ruidos despertaba
with its thousand noises   awakened
el 'pwe ßlo
el pueblo.
the people

'an te‿a 'kel kon 'tras te ðe 'ßi ða‿j
Ante aquel contraste   de vida y
Before that   contrast   of life   and
mis 'te ɾjos
misterios,
mysteries

de 'luθ i   ti 'nje ßlas 'ɟo pen 'se
de luz y   tinieblas, yo pensé
of light and darkness   I   thought
um mo 'men to
un momento:
one moment

'djos 'mi o 'ke   'so los se 'ke ðan loz
¡Dios mío, qué solos   se quedan los
God my   how lonely   remain the
'mwer tos
muertos!
dead

35

oɾa 'θjon de las 'ma ðɾes ke 'tje nen a sus
'i xos em 'bɾa θos

Oración de las madres que tienen a sus hijos en brazos

Prayer of the mothers that hold their sons in arms

'dul θe xe 'sus k(e̯) es 'taz dor 'mi ðo
¡Dulce Jesús, que estás dormido!
Sweet   Jesus   who are   asleep

ˌpoɾ el 'san to 'pe tʃo ke te 'a
¡Por el santo   pecho que te   ha
By   the holy   breast   that you has
(a)ma man 'ta ðo
amamantado,
fed

te   'pi ðo ke (e̯)s te 'i xo 'mi o
te   pido que este hijo mío
you I ask   that this   son my   not
no 'se a sol 'ða ðo
no sea soldado!
be soldier

se lo   ʎe βa 'ɾan   j   'e ɾa
Se lo   llevarán,   ¡y   era
   Him they will take away and he was
'kar ne 'mi a
carne   mía!
flesh   mine

¡Dulce Jesús, que estás dormido!
¡Por el santo pecho que te ha
amamantado,
te pido que este hijo mío no sea
soldado!

Se lo llevarán, ¡y era carne mía!
Me lo matarán, ¡y era mi alegría!
Cuando esté muriendo, dirá:
"¡Madre mía!"
Y yo no sabré la hora ni el día.

¡Dulce Jesús, que estás dormido!
¡Por el santo pecho que te ha
amamantado,
te pido que este hijo mío no sea
soldado!

———————— • ————————

Sweet Jesus who is sleeping
By the holy breast that fed you,
I ask that this son of mine not be
a soldier!

me lo   ma ta 'ɾan j   'e ɾa   mj a le 'ɣɾi a
Me lo   matarán, ¡y   era   mi alegría!
him they will kill   and he was my joy

'kwan do es 'te mu 'ɾjen do ði 'ɾa
Cuando   esté   muriendo, dirá:
When   he is dying   he'll say
'ma ðɾe 'mia
"¡Madre mía!"
Mother   mine

i   'ʝo no sa 'βɾe   la 'o ɾa nj el 'ði a
Y   yo no sabré   la hora ni el día.
And I   not will know the hours nor the day

'dul θe xe 'sus k(e) es 'taz dor 'mi ðo
¡Dulce Jesús, que estás dormido!
Sweet Jesus   who are   asleep

ˌpoɾ el   'san to 'pe tʃo ke   te 'a
¡Por el   santo   pecho   que te   ha
By   the holy   breast   that you has
(a)ma man 'ta ðo
amamantado,
fed

te   'pi ðo ke   (e)s te 'i xo 'mi o
te   pido   que este   hijo mío
you I ask   that this   son my   not
no 'se a sol 'ða ðo
no sea soldado!
be soldier

They'll take him away, and he was
my flesh!
They'll kill him, and he was my
joy!
As he lies dying, he'll say:
"Mother of mine!"
And I will no longer know the
hour or the day.

Sweet Jesus who is sleeping.
By the holy breast that fed you,
I ask that this son of mine not be
a soldier!

36
kan 'θjon an da 'lu θa̱ el 'pan de 'ron da
Canción andaluza: el pan de ronda
Song Andalusian the bread from Ronda

'Awn ke   'to ðo̱   en el 'mun do
Aunque   todo   en el mundo
Even though everything in the world
'fwe se men 'ti ɾa
fuese mentira
were   lie

nos 'ke ða̱ 'es te 'pan mo 'ɾe no tos 'ta ðo
¡nos queda este pan! Moreno, tostado,
to us remains this   bread Brown   toasted

ke 'we le̱ a la 'xa ɾa   ðe 'mon te
que huele a la jara   de monte
that smells like the rockrose of mountain

ke 'sa βe̱ a   βer 'ðað
¡que sabe a   verdad!
that tastes like truth

por   las 'ka ʎes tam 'blaŋ kas tam
Por   las calles tan blancas, tan
Through the streets so white   so
'blaŋ kas
blancas,
white

Aunque todo en el mundo
fuese mentira,
¡nos queda este pan!
Moreno, tostado,
que huele a la jara de monte,
¡que sabe a verdad!

Por las calles tan blancas,
tan blancas,
bajo el cielo azul,
vayamos despacio,
partiendo este pan
¡que sabe a salud!

Y aunque todo en el mundo
fuera mentira,
¡esto no lo es!
Vivamos despacio
la hora que es buena
¡y vengan tristezas después!

———————— • ————————

Even if everything in the world
Were a lie,
We would still have this bread!
Golden, crisp,
Smelling like the mountain
rockrose,
Tasting of truth!

Through the white, white streets
Under the blue sky,
Let us walk slowly,
Sharing this bread
That tastes of health!

'ba xo̯ el   'θje lo̯ a 'θul ba 'ʝa moz
bajo el cielo azul, vayamos
under the sky   blue   let us go
des 'pa θjo
despacio
slowly

par 'tjen do̯ es te 'pan ke   'sa ße̯ a
partiendo   este   pan ¡que sabe   a
sharing   this   bread that tastes like
sa 'luð
salud!
health

j͜   'awŋ ke   'to ðo   en el 'mun do
Y   aunque   todo   en el mundo
And even though everything in the world
'fwe ɾa men 'ti ɾa
fuera   mentira,
were   lie

'es to 'no lo̯ es bi 'ßa moz des 'pa θjo
¡esto no lo es! Vivamos   despacio
this   not it is Let us live slowly

la 'o ɾa k(e̯) 'ez 'bwe na
la hora que es buena
the hour that is   good

i   'ßeŋ gan tris 'te θaz des 'pwes
¡y   vengan   tristezas   después!
and come   sadness   later

Even if everything in the world
Were a lie
This is not one!
Let us live slowly
The hour that is good,
And may the sadness come later.

———Chapter VI

Songs of Mompou

I. *Tres comptines* (1931)

(*Three Ditties*, 1931)

"Tres Comptines" (Three Ditties)

For many Catalans, from the 1880's on Paris was the cultural Mecca; the City of Light not only dictated cultural fashion but was also a place for many Catalan artists to live and work. The cultural alienation due to the persecution of Catalans by the centralist Spanish state in the twentieth century was largely responsible for the move northward.

Mompou is an example of this cultural migration to Paris, and many of his songs were published there by Editions Salabert, among them the first set of *Tres Comptines*, dedicated to Jane Bathori and published in 1931. In 1943 Mompou wrote his second set of "Three Ditties," which was published in 1955, also by Salabert.

To French influence, and particularly to that of Francis Poulenc, we owe the use of children's songs as lyrics for concert pieces. These six ditties are based on rhymes used by children to learn to count and accompany games such as rope-skipping. Two of them, the first and the third, use Catalan texts; the second in each series is in French. The first and third of the second set use Spanish texts. Those in the first set, however, were all given French texts so they could be performed in that language.

We have translated the songs in the least literal manner of this anthology. Obviously they are based more on sound coincidence than on semantic significance.

37
'tɾɛs kom 'ti nəs
Tres comptines
Three ditties

I

'dal duŋ 'ko tʃə nj‿'a‿u nə 'ni nə
Dalt d'un cotxe   n'hi ha una nina
On a   carriage there is a   girl

k(ə)‿ən ɾə 'pi kə (ə)łs kas kə 'βeʎs
que en repica   els cascabells.
who   tolls   the sleigh bells

'tɾɛn tə ku 'ɾan tə
Trenta, quaranta,
thirty   forty

lə 'mɛd ʎə (ə) mər 'ɣan tə
l'ametlla   amarganta,
the almond bitter

əl pi 'ɲɔł mə 'ðu
el   pinyol madur:
the pit   ripe

'bes tən 'tu
ves-te'n tu.
Go away you

Dalt d'un cotxe n'hi ha una nina
que en repica els cascabells.
Trenta, quaranta,
l'ametlla amarganta,
el pinyol madur:
ves-te'n tu.

———————— • ————————

On a buggy there's a girl,
She is ringing the sleigh bells.
Thirty, forty,
The almond is salty,
Its shell is all gray:
You go away!

38

II
Margot la pie a fait son nid
dans la cour à David.
David l'attrappe,
lui coupe la patte;
ric-rac, ric-rac,
comme une patate.
David l'attrappe,
lui coupe la patte;
ric-rac, ric-rac,
comme une patate.

————— • —————

II
Margot the magpie built her nest
In David's courtyard.
David catches her
And cuts off her leg;
ric-rac, ric-rac,
Like a potato.
David catches her
And cuts off her leg,
ric-rac, ric-rac,
Like a potato.

39

III

'e   'βist ˌdins lə 'ʎu nə
He   vist dins la lluna
I have seen inside the moon

'trɛs pə 'tits ku 'niʎs
tres petits conills
three small   rabbits

kə mən 'ʒa ßən 'pɾu nəs
que menjaven prunes
that were eating plums

'kom 'tɾɛz dez bər ɣu 'ɲits
com tres desvergonyits.
like three shameless ones.

lə 'pi pə (ə) lə 'ßo kə
La pipa a la boca
The pipe in the mouth

i lə 'ko pə (ə)lz 'dits
i la copa als dits,
and the glass in the fingers

tot di 'en məs 'tɾɛ sə
Tot dient: "Mestressa,
all saying Mistress

pu 'zɛw nuz uŋ 'got
poseu-nos un got
serve us a glass

ben 'plɛ ðə 'ßi
ben ple de vi."
very full of wine

tot di 'en məs 'tɾɛ sə
tot dient: "Mestressa,
all saying Mistress

pu 'zɛw nuz uŋ 'got
poseu-nos un got
serve us a glass

He vist dins la lluna
tres petits conills
que menjaven prunes
com tres desvergonyits.
La pipa a la boca
i la copa als dits,
tot dient: "Mestressa,
poseu-nos un got
ben ple de vi."
Tot dient: "Mestressa,
poseu-nos un got
ben ple de vi."

⸺⸺⸺ ● ⸺⸺⸺

I saw inside the moon
three little rabbits
Who ate all the plums:
A very bad habit.
In their mouths were pipes,
In their fingers mugs.
They said: "Mistress!
Fill our cups
To the top with wine."
They said: "Mistress!
Fill our cups
To the top with wine!"

⸺⸺⸺ ● ⸺⸺⸺

French Versions:
I
Sur un coche y a une belle
qui fait sonner les grelots.
Trente, quarante, l'amère l'amande,
le dur noyau mûr. Va-t'en toi.

ben 'plɛ ðə 'ßi
ben ple de vi."
very full of wine

III

J'ai vu dans la lune
Trois petits lapins
qui mangaient des prunes
comme des petits coquins.
La pipe à la bouche,
le verre à la main,
En disant: Mes dames,
versez nous du vin,
du vin tout plein.
En disant: Mes dames,
versez nous du vin,
du vin tout plein.

II. *Tres comptines* (1943)

(*Three Ditties*, 1943)

"Aserrín, Aserrán" (Ric-ric-ric, Rac-rac-rac)
"Petitte fille de Paris" (Little Girl from Paris)
"Pito, pito, colorito" (Pito, Pito, Full of Colors)

40
a se 'rin a se 'ran
Aserrín, Aserrán
Ric-ric-ric Rac-rac-rac

a se 'rin a se 'ran loz ma 'ðe ɾoz de
Aserrín, aserrán, los maderos   de
Aserrín, aserrán, the logs   of

ˌsaŋ 'xwan
San Juan.
Saint John.

loz de a 'ri βa 'sje ran 'bjen i   loz
Los de arriba sierran bien y   los
The of above   saw   well and the

de a 'βa xo tam 'bjen
de abajo   también.
of beneath also

al   mi 'la no 'ke le 'ðan
Al   milano, ¿qué le dan?
To the kite bird what him they give?

be ʎo 'ti tas ˌkon el 'pan
Bellotitas   con   el   pan.
Little acorns with the bread

Aserrín, aserrán,
los maderos de San Juan.
Los de arriba sierran bien
y los de abajo también.
Al milano, ¿qué le dan?
Bellotitas con el pan.
Por la noche pan y pera,
y otra noche pera y pan.
Al milano, ¿qué le dan?
Bellotitas con el pan.
Por la noche pan y pera
y otra noche pera y pan.
Aserrín, aserrán,
los maderos de San Juan.

———————— • ————————

por la 'no tʃe pan   i   'pe ɾa j
Por la noche pan y   pera, y
By the night bread and pear and
'o tɾa 'no tʃe 'pe ɾa j   'pan
otra noche pera y   pan.
other night pear and bread

al   mi 'la no 'ke le   'ðan
Al   milano, ¿qué le dan?
To the kite bird what him they give?
be ʎo 'ti tas ˌkon el 'pan
Bellotitas   con el pan.
Little acorns with the bread

por la 'no tʃe pan   i   'pe ɾa j
Por la noche pan y   pera, y
By the night bread and pear and
'o tɾa 'no tʃe 'pe ɾa j   'pan
otra noche pera y   pan.
other night pear and bread

a se 'rin a se 'ran loz ma 'ðe ɾoz de
Aserrín, aserrán, los maderos   de
Aserrín, aserrán, the logs   of
ˌsaŋ 'xwan
San Juan.
Saint John.

Ric-ric-ric, rac-rac-rac,
The logs of Saint John.
Those on top, I can saw;
Those on bottom, I can too.
What do they feed the kite bird?
Little acorns with his bread.
At night bread with pears,
The next night pears with bread.
What do they feed the kite bird?
Little acorns with his bread.
At night bread with pears,
The next night pears with bread.
Ric-ric-ric, rac-rac-rac,
The logs of Saint John.

41
Petite fille de Paris
Little girl from Paris

Petite fille de Paris,
prête-moi tes souliers gris.
Prête-moi tes souliers gris
pour aller en Paradis.
Nous irons un à un
dans le chemin des Saints,
deux à deux
dans le chemin des cieux.
Prête-moi tes soulers gris
pour aller en Paradis.
Nous irons un à un
dans le chemin des Saints,
deux à deux
dans le chemin des cieux.

———— • ————

Little girl from Paris
Lend me your gray shoes.
Lend me your gray shoes
To go to Paradise.
We shall go, one by one,
On the pathway of the saints.
We shall go, two by two,
On the pathway in the sky.
Lend me your gray shoes
To go to Paradise.
We shall go, one by one,
On the pathway of the saints.
We shall go, two by two,
On the pathway in the sky.

42
'pi to 'pi to ˌko lo 'ɾi to
Pito, pito, colorito
Pito, pito, full of colors

'pi to 'pi to ˌko lo 'ɾi to
Pito, pito, colorito,
Pito, pito, full of colors,

'don de 'βas   'tu ˌtam bo 'ni to
¿dónde vas   tú   tan   bonito?
where   you go you so   pretty

'pi to 'pi to ˌko lo 'ɾi to
Pito, pito, colorito,
Pito, pito, full of colors,

'don de 'βas   'tu ˌtam bo 'ni to
¿dónde vas   tú   tan   bonito?
where   you go you so   pretty

ˌa la (a) 'θe ɾa βer ða 'ðe ɾa
A la acera   verdadera.
To the sidewalk true

'pim 'pom 'fwe ɾa
Pim, pom, fuera.
Pim pom out

Pito, pito, colorito,
¿dónde vas tú tan bonito?
Pito, pito, colorito,
¿dónde vas tú tan bonito?
A la acera
verdadera.
Pim, pom, fuera.

———————— • ————————

Pito, pito, full of colors,
Where are you going, you so
prettty?
Pito, pito, full of colors,
Where are you going, you so
pretty?
To the sidewalk,
But don't talk:
One, two, three!

III. *Combat del somni*

(*Dream Combat*)

"Damunt de tu només les flors" (Over You Only the Flowers)
"Aquesta nit un mateix vent" (Tonight Only One Wind)
"Jo et pressentia com la mar" (I Had a Premonition of You Like the Sea)

This short cycle was published between 1946 and 1949 by Editions Salabert in Paris. It is based on three compositions from the book of sonnets *Combat del somni* (Dream Combat) by Josep Janés (1913–1959), published originally in 1937 by Janés's own Edicions de la Rosa dels Vents. The poems were written after the death of a beloved of the poet, a woman called Maria Victòria. But it was surely the dreamy, simple, and abstract quality of the verses that attracted Mompou.

Of all the poetic styles in the lyrics of Mompou's songs, these elegantly streamlined but conceptually ambitious pieces of what was hopefully called "pure poetry" are the closest to the style of Mompou's music.

43
də 'mun də 'tu nu 'mez las 'flɔs
Damunt de tu només les flors
Over you only the flowers

də 'mun də 'tu nu 'mez ləs 'flɔs
Damunt de tu   només les flors.
Over   you only   the flowers

'e ɾən   ˌkom u nə̯ u̯ 'frɛ nə 'βlaŋ kə
Eren   com una ofrena   blanca:
They were like   an   offer   white

Damunt de tu només les flors.
Eren com una ofrena blanca:
la llum que daven al teu cos
mai més seria de la branca;

tota una vida de perfum
amb el seu bes t'era donada.
Tu resplendies de la llum
per l'esguard clos atresorada.

lə ˈʎum kə ˈða βən əɫ ˈtew ˈkɔs
la llum que daven al teu cos
the light that they gave to your body

ˈmaj ˈmes sə ˈɾi ə ðə lə ˈβɾaŋ kə
mai més seria de la branca;
ever more it would be of the branch

ˈto tə̯ u̯ nə ˈβi ðə ðə pəɾ ˈfum
tota una vida de perfum
all a life of perfume

ˌəm əɫ sew ˈβes ˈte ɾə du ˈna ðə
amb el seu best' era donada.
with the their kiss you it was given

ˈtu ɾəs plən ˈdi əz ðə lə ˈʎum
Tu resplendies de la llum
You shone of the light

pəɾ ləz ˈɣwart ˈklɔz ə tɾə zu ˈɾa ðə
per l' esguard clos atresorada.
by the look closed treasured

sj ə ˈɣes pu ˈɣut ˈe sə sus ˈpir
¡Si hagués pogut ésser sospir
If I had been able to be sigh

də ˈflɔ du ˈnar mə ˌkom un ˈʎiɾ
de flor! Donar-me, com un llir,
of flower to give myself as a lily

ə ˈtu pəɾ ˈkɛ lə ˈme βə ˈβi ðə
a tu, perquè la meva vida
to you so that the my life

¡Si hagués pogut ésser sospir
de flor! Donar-me, com un llir,
a tu, perquè la meva vida

s'anés marcint sobre el teu pit.
I no saber mai més la nit,
que al teu costat fóra esvaïda.

———— • ————

Over you only the flowers.
They were like a white offering:
The light they threw on your body
Would never again be the same as
that of the branch;

They gave you a whole life of
perfume
With their kisses.
You were resplendent in the light
Kept as a treasure by your closed
eyes.

If I could have been the sigh
Of a flower! Offer myself, as a lily,
To you, so that my life

Would wither over your breast.
And no longer know the night
That, next to you, would have
vanished.

sə 'nez   mər 'sin   'so βɾə (ə)ɫ
s' anés   marcint   sobre el
itself it went withering over   the
'tew 'pit
teu pit.
your breast

i   'no sə 'βe   'maj 'mez lə 'nit
I   no saber   mai més la nit,
and not to know ever more the night

k(ə) əl   'tew kus 'tat 'fo ɾə
que al   teu costat fóra
that to the your side   it would be
(ə)z βə 'i ðə
esvaïda.
vanished

44
ə 'kɛs tə 'nit um mə 'teʃ 'ben
Aquesta nit un mateix vent
This night a same wind

ə 'kəz tə 'nit um mə 'teʃ 'ben
Aquesta nit un mateix vent
This   night a   same   wind

j 'u nə mə 'te ʃə 'βɛ lə (ə)n 'sɛ zə
i   una mateixa vela encesa
and a   same   sail   lighted

də 'βi ən 'du əɫ tew pen sə 'men
devien   dur el teu pensament
must have taken the your thought

Aquesta nit un mateix vent
i una mateixa vela encesa
devien dur el teu pensament
i el meu per mars on la tendresa

es torna música i cristall.
El bes se'ns feia transparència
—si tu eres l'aigua, jo el
mirall—
com si abracéssim una absència.

j‿əl 'mew pər   'marz ˌon   lə
i el meu per   mars on   la
and the mine through seas where the
tən 'drə zə
tendresa
tenderness

əs 'tor nə 'mu zi kə j kris 'taʎ
es torna   música i   cristall.
itself becomes music   and crystal

əl 'βes səns 'fɛ jə trəns pə 'rɛn si ə
El bes se'ns feia   transparència
The kiss itself to us made luminosity

si 'tu 'e rəz 'ləj ɣwə 'ʒɔ‿əl mi 'raʎ
—si tu eres l'aigua, jo el mirall—
if   you were the water I the mirror

'kom sj ə βrə 'se sim 'u nə (ə)p 'sɛn si ə
com si abracéssim una absència.
as   if we embraced an   absence

əl 'nos trə 'sɛɫ 'fo rə   put 'se
¿El nostre cel   fóra,   potser,
The our   heaven would be perhaps

un 'som ni ə 'tɛrn ə 'ʃi ðə 'βe zuz
un somni etern, així, de besos
a dream eternal thus of kisses

'fets mə lu 'ði ə j 'un no 'se
fets melodia, i un no ser
made melody   and a not being

¿El nostre cel fóra, potser,
un somni etern, així, de besos
fets melodia, i un no ser
de cossos junts i d'ulls encesos

amb flames blanques, i un sospir
d'acariciar sedes de llir?

———————— ● ————————

Tonight only one wind
And only one burning sail
Are carrying your thought
And mine across seas on which
tenderness

Becomes music and crystal.
Our kiss became a luminosity
—You were the water, I the
mirror—
As if we were embracing an
absence.

Is our heaven, perhaps,
An eternal dream of kisses
Made melody, and a not being
Of bodies together and eyes
burning

With white flames, and a sigh
As if caressing silken lilies?

de 'ko sus 'ʒunz   i   'ð u ʎz ən 'sɛ zuz
de cossos junts   i   d' ulls encesos
of bodies together and of eyes lighted

əm 'fla məz 'βlaŋ kəz j⌢un sus 'pir
amb flames blanques, i ‿ un sospir
with flames white   and a sigh

də ˌkə ɾi si 'a 'sɛ ðəz ðə 'ʎiɾ
d' acariciar sedes de llir?
of caressing silks   of lily?

45

'ʒɔ ət pɾə sən 'ti ə 'kom lə 'maɾ
Jo et pressentia com la mar
I you foreboded like the sea

'ʒɔ⌢ət   pɾə sən 'ti ə 'kom lə 'maɾ
Jo et   pressentia com la mar
I   you foreboded like the sea

i   'kom əl 'βen im 'men sə 'ʎiw ɾə
i   com el vent, immensa, lliure,
and like the wind immense   free

'ał tə ðə 'mun də 'tot ət 'zaɾ
alta, damunt de tot atzar
tall above   of all fate

i   'tod dəs 'ti j⌢ən əl 'mew 'βiw ɾə
i   tot destí. I en el meu viure,
and all destiny and in the my   living

Jo et pressentia com la mar
i com el vent, immensa, lliure,
alta, damunt de tot atzar
i tot destí. I en el meu viure,

com el respir. I ara que et tinc
veig com el somni et limitava.
Tu no ets un nom, ni un gest. No vinc
a tu com a la imatge blava

d'un somni humà. Tu no ets la mar,
que és presonera dins de platges,
tu no ets el vent, pres en l'espai.

Tu no tens límits; no hi ha, encar,
mots per a dir-te, ni paisatges
per ser el teu món—ni hi seran mai.

'kom əl rəs 'piɾ i   'a ɾə kə (ə)t 'tiŋ
com el respir. I   ara que et tinc
like   the breathing And now that you I have

'bɛtʃ kom əl 'som ni ət li mi 'ta βə
veig com el somni et limitava.
I see how the dream   you limited

'tu no 'etz un 'nɔm nj un 'ʒest
Tu no ets un nom, ni un gest.
You not are a   name nor a   gesture

no 'βiŋ
No vinc
Not I come

ə 'tu 'kom ə lə j 'ma dʒə 'βla βə
a tu com a la imatge blava
to you like to the image   blue

dun 'som ni u 'ma 'tu no 'ets lə 'mar
d' un somni humà. Tu no ets la mar,
of a dream   human You not are the sea

k(ə) 'es prə zu 'ne ɾə ðins ðə 'pla dʒəz
que és presonera   dins de platges,
which is prisoner   inside of beaches

'tu no 'ets əł 'βen 'prɛz ən ləs 'paj
tu no ets el vent, pres en l' espai.
You not are the wind caught in the space

'tu no 'tens 'li mits no j 'a ən 'kar
Tu no tens límits; ni hi ha, encar,
You not have limits Not there is   yet

I had a premonition of you being
like the sea
And the wind: Immense, free,
Towering over all fate
And all destiny. And in my life

Like breathing. But now that I
have you
I see how limiting my dream had
been.
You are not a name nor a gesture.
Nor do I come
To you as one goes to the bluish
image

Of a human dream. You are not
the sea,
For the sea is a prisoner held
captive by beaches;
You are not the wind, caught in
space.

You have no limits; there are yet
No words to name you, no scenery
To become your world—there
never will be.

'mots pəɾ ə 'ðir tə   ni   paj 'za dʒəz
mots per a dir- te,   ni   paisatges
words to   call you nor views

pəɾ se (ə)ɬ 'tew 'mon ni
per ser el   teu   món —ni hi
to   be the your world nor there
sə 'ɾan 'maj
seran   mai.
will be ever

IV. *Quatre mélodies*

(*Four Melodies*)

"Incertitud" (Uncertainty)
"Rosa del camí" (Rose of the Path)
"Neu" (Snow)
"Cortina de fullatge" (Curtain of Leaves)

Four poetic sketches form the basis of this song cycle. The composer himself wrote the texts, in the style of the "pure poetry" of the thirties.

The themes seem to be favorites of Mompou: The speaker of the verses is expectant, in the night, of what destiny holds for him. The images are simple and speak of pathways, of the night sky, of flowers.

46
in sər ti 'tut
Incertitud
Uncertainty

in sər ti 'tud dəɫ   'mew kə 'mi
Incertitud   del   meu camí.
Uncertainty of the my   road

dəɫ   'mew ə 'mor 'tot lim fi 'nit
Del   meu amor tot l' infinit,
Of the my   love   all   the infinite

dəs 'tre ʎəs nəs 'ta (ə)s 'krit
d' estrelles n' està escrit.
of stars   it is   written

Incertitud del meu camí.
Del meu amor tot l'infinit,
d'estrelles n'està escrit.
Claror dels camps, claror de nit.
Claror de cel, sobre un desig.

———————— • ————————

Uncertainty of my path.
All the infinity of my love
Is written in the stars.
Light of the fields, light of the night.
Light of the sky over my wish.

klə 'ɾo ðəls 'kaɲs klə 'ɾo ðə 'nit
Claror dels camps, claror de nit.
Clarity of the fields   clarity of night

klə 'ɾo ðəl   'sɛl 'so βɾə̯un də 'zitʃ
Claror del   cel, sobre un desig.
Clarity of the sky over   a   wish.

47
'ɾɔ zə ðəɫ ka 'mi
Rosa del cami
Rose on the path

ən 'doɫz dəz 'maj
En dolç desmai
In sweet swoon

du 'ɾan lə 'nit
durant la nit
during the night

ə 'so βɾə ðəl   'βɔsk
a sobre del   bosc
on top   of the forest

ə kəj 'ɣut u n(ə) əs 'tɾɛ ʎə
ha caigut una   estrella.
has fallen a   star

də 'βɔm mə 'ti
De bon matí
Of good morning

En dolç desmai
durant la nit
a sobre del bosc
ha caigut una estrella.
De bon matí
jo trobaré una rosa
sobre el meu camí.

────────── • ──────────

With a sweet swoon
During the night
A star has fallen
On the forest.
Early in the morning
I will find a rose
On my path.

'ʒɔ tɾu βə 'rɛ̯w nə 'rɔ zə
jo trobaɾe una rosa
I   shall find a   rose

'so βɾə (ə)ł 'mew kə 'mi
Sobre el meu camí.
Over   the my   path

48
'new
Neu
Snow

'nɔ̯es 'new 'sɔɲ 'flɔz ðə 'sɛł
No és neu, són flors de cel.
Not it is snow it's flowers of sky

'kɔr 'mew kom tə ðəz 'fu ʎəs
Cor meu com te desfulles.
Heart mine how you you unleave

'sɔɲ 'fuʎz ðə mə 'βi ðə (ə)s kin 'sats
Són fulls de ma vida esquinçats.
It's pages from my life   torn

plu 'ʒɛ tə ðə pə 'pe 'βlaŋ
Plugeta de paper blanc.
Little rain of paper white

'nɔ̯es 'new 'sɔɲ 'flɔz ðə 'sɛł
No és neu, són flors de cel.
Not it is snow it's flowers of sky

No és neu, són flors de cel.
Cor meu com te desfulles.
Són fulls de ma vida esquinçats.
Plugeta de paper blanc.
No és neu, són flors de cel.
Dolor, com te desfulles.
Ai! Quina tristesa fa.

———————————— • ————————————

Not snow but flowers from the
sky.
Oh, my heart, how you're
unleaving.
Pages from my life, all torn to
pieces,
Like rain made out of white paper.
Not snow, but flowers from the
sky.
Oh, my suffering, how you're
unleaving.
Oh, how sad it is!

du 'lo 'koŋ tə ðəz 'fu ʎəs
Dolor, com te desfulles.
Pain how you you unleave

'aj 'ki nə tris 'tɛ zə 'fa
Ai! quina tristesa fa.
Ah! what sadness it makes

49
kur 'ti nə ðə fu 'ʎa dʒə
Cortina de fullatge
Curtain of leaves

ən 'ka ɾə 'βɛtʃ əl ʎuɲ
Encara veig al lluny
Still I see at the far

əłz 'ʎumz ðə mə siw 'tat
els llums de ma ciutat.
the lights of my city

j əł 'nɔs tɾə pə 'tid 'niw
I el nostre petit niu
And the our small nest

ə mə 'ɣat 'en tɾə (ə)ł ɾə 'ma dʒə
amagat entre el ramatge.
hidden amidst the branches

'se kə lə 'ʎu nə
Sé que la lluna
I know that the moon

Encara veig al lluny
els llums de ma ciutat.
I el nostre petit niu
Amagat entre el ramatge.

Sé que la lluna
és al darrera d'aquests arbres.
I en la penombra d'aquest bosc
jo puc fer entrar
una carícia de llum tendra sobre els
teus ulls
tan sols obrint una cortina de
fullatge.

———————— • ————————

I can still see, far away,
The lights of my city.
And our little nest
Hidden in between branches.

'ez əɫ ðə 're ɾə ðə 'kɛ   'dza βɾəz
és al darrera d' aquests arbres.
is   to the back of these   trees

j͜   ən lə   pə 'nom βɾə ðə 'kɛt   'bɔsk
I   en la   penombra   d' aquest bosc
And in the penumbra   of this   forest

'ʒɔ 'pug 'fe͜   (ə)n 'tɾaɾ
jo puc fer   entrar
I   can   make enter

u nə kə 'ɾi si ə ðə 'ʎum 'tɛn ðɾə
una carícia   de llum tendra
a   caress   of light tender

'so βɾə (ə)ɫz 'tewz 'uʎs
sobre els   teus ulls
over the   your eyes

'tan 'sɔɫz u 'βɾin   u nə kur 'ti nə
tan sols obrint   una cortina
    only opening a   curtain

ðə fu 'ʎa dʒə
de fullatge.
of leaves

I know that the moon
Is behind these trees.
And in the shadows of this forest
I can let in
A tender caress of light for your eyes
If only I open a curtain of leaves.

V. *Cançons diverses*

(*Various Songs*)

"Cançó de la fira" (Song of the Fair)
"Cançoneta incerta" (Song of Uncertainty)
"L'hora grisa" (The Gray Hour)
"Sant Martí" (Sant Martí)
"Aureana do sil" (Golden Girl of the Sil)

We have gathered under the title *Cançons diverses* four Catalan songs of Mompou and have appended to the group one song in Galician, a sister language of Portuguese spoken in the northwestern region of Spain. We do not mean to claim any stylistic unity by gathering them in this section, but simply to avoid a confusing proliferation of pages and subdivisions.

Cançó de la fira, "Song of the Fair", was published by Editions Salabert in Paris in 1949. It follows the text of the poem by Tomàs Garcés in his neo-populist style. The poem takes almost literally the metaphoric wonders offered by a county fair. A poetic and childlike acceptance of the imaginative is dear to Mompou.

Cançoneta incerta, "Song of Uncertainty", deals with two equal favorites among the composer's themes: uncertainty and the metaphor of the path or roadway. It was published in 1953 in Madrid by Unión Musical Española, and Mompou dedicated it to the memory of the lyric soprano Maria Barrientos (1884–1946). The text is taken from the great Catalan poet Josep Carner (1884–1970), again in one of his most populist veins.

The same publisher issued, one year later, in 1954, *L'hora grisa*, "The Gray Hour". It is dedicated to Helise Paris de Blancafort, and its text is a poem by that lady's husband, Manuel Blancafort. The same themes dear to Mompou appear here.

The fourth song is from a later period; it was published in Barcelona by Edicions Tenora in 1982 and is dedicated to the contralto Anna Ricci (b. 1930). The poem makes reference to a Cistercian monastery devoted to St. Martin. The monastery itself is a beautiful Romanesque building set deep in the

Pyrenean region of Cerdanya, near Mount Canigó, in northern Catalonia (today within the boundaries of France). The poem seems to refer alternately to the monastery and to the saint himself. St. Martin was the most popular of the warrior-saints among the Catalans; his better known (and not altogether unpuzzling) deed was sharing his cloak with a beggar by slitting the precious robe down the middle with his sword. Many Catalan towns are named after Saint Martin, attesting to his early reputation; so is of course the monastery at the foot of Canigó, an impressive granite ("eye of serpent" in the popular Catalan phrase) structure. It is traditional to gather periodically at monasteries for pilgrimages, thus the reference to "the pen" (there are poetry readings during these pilgrimages), and "the wine" (the pilgrimage always ends with a celebration). In this poem, however, there seems to be a confusion with another warrior-saint, St. George, the famous slayer of the dragon. In the late Middle Ages St. George became the patron saint of chivalry and eventually of Catalonia (as well as England). The line referring to the serpent and its poison springs out of that confusion.

The song based on the Galician poem by Ramón Cabanillas repeats the words of its title, *Aureana do Sil. Aureana* is a feminine form and of course means a woman; it also has the root *aur*, "gold". We have translated it only in the title and have left the original line in the song throughout our version in order to avoid, well, sounding silly. Sil is the most important river in Galicia. We have not heard of any gold discovered there in many centuries; the cautionary remarks of the poet must be rather well founded. The poem is a modern learned rendering of a genre called *pastorella* discussed elsewhere in this anthology.

50
kən 'so ðə lə 'fi ɾə
Cançó de la fira
Song of the fair

əɫs sews tɾə 'zoɾz 'mos tɾə lə   'fi ɾə
Els seus tresors mostra la fira
Its   treasures shows   the fair

pər 'kɛ (ə)ɫz ə 'ɣa fis əm   lə   'ma
perquè els   agafis   amb la   mà.
So that them you take with the hand

ˌʒɔ 'sok kən 'sad də 'tam   mi 'ɾaɾ
Jo sóc cansat de tant   mirar
I   am tired   of so much looking

i   lə 'me β(ə) 'a ni mə sus 'pi ɾə
i   la meva   ànima   sospira.
and the my   soul   sighs

ku 'to ðə 'su kɾə kə βə 'ʎɛts
Cotó de sucre, cavallets,
Cotton of sugar, merry-go-round,

'kan tiz də 'βi ðɾə j   ə ɾə 'ka ðəs
càntirs de vidre i   arracades
vessels of glass   and earrings

'ʎu ən i   'sal tən 'fen   bə 'ʎa ðəs
lluen i   salten fent   ballades
glisten and jump   making dances

'en tɾə (ə)l βru 'ʒid dəls   plə tə 'ɾɛts
entre el brogit dels   platerets.
among the noise   of the cymbals

Els seus tresors mostra la fira
perquè els agafis amb la mà.
Jo sóc cansat de tant mirar
i la meva ànima sospira.
Cotó de sucre, cavallets,
càntirs de vidre i arracades
lluen i salten fent ballades
entre el brogit dels platerets.
El teu esguard ple d'avidesa
un immortal desig el mou.
¿Cerques un espectacle nou
més amunt de la fira encesa?
Els estels punxen tot el cel.
L'oreig escampa espurnes. Mira:
cam poc a poc es mor la fira
sota la llum d'aquell estel.
Glateixes per copsar l'estrella?
Ai, que el desig t'estreny el cor!
Mai més voldràs la joia d'or
ni la rialla del titella.

əl tew əz 'ɣwar 'plɛ ðə βi 'ðɛ zə
El teu esguard ple d' avidesa
    your gaze   full of eagerness

un im mur 'tal ðə 'zitʃ əl 'mow
un immortal desig el mou.
an immortal   desires it moves

'sɛr kəz   un əs pək 'ta klə 'nɔw
¿Cerques   un espectacle nou
Are you looking for a   spectacle   new

'mez ə 'mun də lə 'fi rə (ə)n 'sɛ zə
més amunt de la fira encesa?
more upwards of the fair   glowing

əlz əs 'tɛls 'pun ʃən 'tot əl 'cɛl
Els estels punxen tot el cel.
The stars   pierce   all   the sky

lu 'rɛtʃ əs 'kaɱ pə (ə)s 'pur nəs mi ɾa
L' oreig escampa espurnes.   Mira
The breeze scatters   sparkles   Look

kaɱ 'pok ə 'pok əz 'mor lə 'fi ɾə
com poc a poc es mor la fira
how little by little itself dies the fair

'so tə lə 'ʎum də 'keʎ əs 'tɛl
sota la llum d' aquell estel.
under the light of that   star

glə 'tɛ ʃəs   pər kup 'sa ləs 'tɾe ʎə
Glateixes   per copsar l' estrella?
Do you throb for catching the star

The fair displays its wonders
So you can grab them with your hands.
I am tired of only looking
And my soul wants to sigh.
Cotton candy, merry-go-rounds,
Vessels of glass, and earrings
Glisten and jump with their dances
Among the clamor of cymbals.
Your gaze, filled with eagerness,
Follows an immortal wish.
Are you seeking a new spectacle
Beyond the glowing fair?
The stars are piercing the sky;
The breeze scatters the sparkles.
Look:
Little by little the fair dies
Under the light of that star.
Does your heart throb to catch that star?
Ah, desire chokes your heart!
Never again will you wish for the golden jewel
Or the laughter of the clown.

'aj kə (ə)ł ðə 'zitʃ təs 'trɛɲ ə̣ł 'kcr
Ai, que el desig t' estreny el cor!
Ah the desire you it clutches the heart

ˌmaj 'mez buł 'ðras lə 'ʒɔ jə 'ðɔr
Mai més voldràs la joia d' or
Never more you'll want the jewel of gold

ni lə ri 'a ʎə ðəł ti 'te ʎə
ni la rialla del titella.
nor the laughter of the marionette

51
kən su 'nɛ ta in 'sɛr tə
Cançoneta incerta
Little song uncertain

ə 'kɛ̣t kə 'mi taɱ 'fi taɱ 'fi ki
Aquest camí tan fi, tan fi, qui
This trail so fine so fine who

'sap on 'mɛ ŋə
sap on mena?
knows where it goes?

'ez ə lə 'ßi lə o 'ez al 'pi
Es a la vila o és al pi
Is it to the town or is it to the pine

ðə lə kə 'rɛ nə
de la carena?
of the mountain

Aquest camí tan fi, tan fi,
qui sap on mena?
Es a la vila o és al pi
de la carena?

Un lliri blau color de cel
diu "vine, vine";
però "no passis" diu un vel
de teranyina.

¿Serà drecera del gosat,
rossola ingrata
o bé un camí d'enamorat
colgat de mata?

¿Es un recer per a dormir
qui passi pena?
Aquest camí tan fi, tan fi,
qui sap on mena?

un 'ʎi ɾi 'βlaw ku 'lo ðə 'sɛɫ 'ðiw
Un lliri blau color de cel diu
A lily blue color of sky says

'βi nə 'βi nə
"vine, vine";
Come, come

pə 'ɾɔ no 'pa siz 'diw um 'bɛɫ ðə tə ɾə 'ɲi nə
però "no passis" diu un vel de teranyina.
but not pass says a veil of gossamer

sə 'ɾa ðɾə 'se ɾə ðəl ɣu 'zat
¿Serà drecera del gosat,
Will it be shortcut of the daring

ru 'sɔ lạ in 'gɾa tə
rossola ingrata
heath ungrateful

o 'βe un kə 'mi ðə nə mu 'ɾat kul 'ɣad
o bé un camí d'enamorat colgat
or else a trail of lover covered

də 'ma tə
de mata?
with brush

'ez un ɾə 'se pəɾ ə ðuɾ 'mi ki 'pa si
¿Es un recer per a dormir qui passi
Is it a shelter to sleep who passes

'pɛ nə
pena?
pain

¿Qui sap si trist o somrient
acull a l'hoste?
Qui sap si mor sobtadament
sota la brosta?

¿Qui sabia[10] mai aquest camí,
a què em convida?
I és camí incert cada matí,
n'és cada vida,
n'és cada vida.[11]

————— • —————

This path so fine, so fine,
where will it take us?
To town or to that pine
There on the mountain?

A sky blue lily
says: "come, come";
But "go no further" says a veil
Of gossamer.

Is this a shortcut for the brave,
Ungrateful heath,
Or is it a trail for one in love
All dense with brush?

Is it a shelter for the sleep
Of one in pain?
This path so fine, so fine
Where will it take us?

Who knows if sad, or with a smile,
It welcomes the traveler?
Who knows if it dies all of a
sudden
Under the thicket?

ə 'kɛt   kə 'mi taɱ 'fi   taɱ fi   ki
Aquest camí   tan fi,   tan fi,   qui
This   trail   so fine so   fine who

'sap   on   'mɛ nə
sap   on   mena?
knows where it goes?

Who would ever know this path?
What does it invite me to?
An uncertain road is every
morning,
and every life,
and every life.

ki   'sap   si 'trist o sum ri 'en
Qui sap   si trist o somrient
Who knows if sad   or smiling

ə 'kuʎ ə   'los tə
acull a   l' hoste?
it welcomes the guest?

ki   'sap   si 'mɔr sub 'ta ðə 'men
¿Qui sap   si mor sobtadament
Who knows if it dies suddenly

'so tə lə 'βrɔs tə
sota la brosta?
under the thicket?

ki   sə 'βi ə 'maj ə 'kɛt kə 'mi ə 'kɛ (ə)m
¿Qui sabia mai aquest camí a qué em
Who knew   ever this   trail   to what me

kum 'βi ðə
convida?
it invites?

j 'es kə 'mi in 'sɛrt 'ka ðə mə 'ti
I és camí incert   cada matí,
And it is trail uncertain each morning,

'nes 'ka ðə 'βi ðə 'nes ka ða 'βi ðə
n'és cada vida, n'és cada vida.
it is each   life, it is each life

52

'lɔ ɾə 'ɣɾi zə
L'hora grisa
The hour gray

'tod 'dɔrm ə 'lɔ ɾə   'ɣɾi zə
Tot dorm a l' hora   grisa,
All   sleeps in the hour gray

əɫz 'a βɾəs ləs mun 'ta ɲəs əɫz u 'seʎs
els arbres, les muntanyes, els ocells,
the trees   the mountains   the birds
əɫ 'βen
el vent!
the wind

ˌSɔ lə 'men ɔɫ 'fum 'fa   sun kə 'mi
Solament el fum fa   son camí
Only   the smoke makes its   way
ˌlen tə 'men
lentament,
slowly

ə 'mun ə 'mun ˌkom lu ɾə 'sjo
amunt, amunt, com l' oració.
upward upward like   the prayer

ˌmes 'tart kwan əɫ 'sɛɫ sə 'pa ɣi
Més tard, quan el cel s' apagui,
More late   when the sky itself extinguishes

sur ti 'ɾa ‿ u nə‿(ə)s tɾe 'ʎɛ tə 'ðɔɾ
sortirà   una estrelleta d' or.
it will come out a little star   of gold

Tot dorm a l'hora grisa,
els arbres, les muntanyes, els ocells,
el vent!
Solament el fum fa son camí
lentament,
amunt, amunt, com l'oració.
Més tard, quan el cel s'apagui,
sortirà una estrelleta d'or.
Tot dorm a l'hora grisa,
els arbres, les muntanyes, els ocells,
el vent!

———————— • ————————

All is asleep in the gray hour,
The trees, the mountains, the
birds, the wind!
Only the smoke makes its way
slowly
Upwards, upwards, like a prayer.
Later, when the sky grows darker,
A little golden star will appear.
All is asleep in the gray hour,
The trees, the mountains, the
birds, the wind!

'tod 'dɔrm ə 'lɔ ɾə   'ɣɾi zə
Tot dorm a l' hora   grisa,
All   sleeps in the hour gray

əłz 'a βɾəs ləs mun 'ta ɲəs əłz u 'seʎs
els arbres, les muntanyes, els ocells,
the trees   the mountains   the birds

əł 'βen
el vent!
the wind

53
'sam mər 'ti
Sant Martí
Saint Martin

'pe ðɾə 'fɛr mə (ə)n tɾə mun 'ta ɲəs
Pedra ferma entre   muntanyes.
Stone firm   amidst mountains

'uʎ də 'serp u 'lo   ðə 'pi
Ull de serp, olor   de pi.
Eye of snake fragrance of pine

'sam mər 'ti 'rej ðə ləs 'te βəz ən 'tɾa ɲəz
Sant Martí, rei   de les teves   entranyes,
Saint Martin king of the your   entrails

lə 'plo mə 'laj ɾə j⌣ əł 'βi
la ploma, l' aire i   el vi.
the pen   the air and the wine

rəs 'pi ɾə lə 'te βə j 'ma dʒə
Respira   la teva   imatge
It breathes the your image

Pedra ferma entre muntanyes.
Ull de serp, olor de pi.
Sant Martí,
rei de les teves entranyes,
la ploma, l'aire i el vi.

Respira la teva imatge
caritat pel pelegrí.
Sant Martí,
la intimitat del paisatge,
tu i jo pel mateix camí.

Cavaller del Crist, l'espasa
mati el serpent i el verí.
Sant Martí,
vetlli la flama la casa
i la veu del Sinaí.

kə ɾi 'tat pəł   pə lə 'ɣɾi
caritat pel   pelegrí.
charity   for the pilgrim

'sam mər 'ti lə͜ jn ti mi 'tad dəł
Sant Martí, la intimitat   del
Saint Martin the intimateness of the
pəj 'za dʒə
paisatge,
view

'tu͜ j   'ʒɔ pəł   mə 'teʃ kə 'mi
tu i   jo pel   mateix camí.
you and I   on the same   road

kə βə 'ʎe ðəł   'kɾist ləs 'pa zə
Cavaller del   Crist, l' espasa
Knight   of the Christ the sword

'ma tj əł sər 'pen j͜ əł βə 'ɾi
mati el serpent i   el verí.
kill   the serpent and the poison

'sam mər 'ti 'βed ʎi   lə 'fla mə lə
Sant Martí, vetlli   la flama la
Saint Martin let it guard the flame   the
'ka zə
casa
house

i   lə 'βɛw ðəł   si nə 'i
i   la veu del   Sinaí.
and the voice of the Sinai.

Firm stone amidst mountains.
Granite stone, fragrance of pine.
Sant Martí,
King in the very core,
The pen, the air, and the wine.

Your image breathes
Compassion for the pilgrim.
Sant Martí,
The intimacy of your
surroundings,
You and I on the same road.

Knight of the Christ, let your
sword
Kill the monster and its poison.
Sant Martí,
Let your flame guard the house
And the voice of Sinai.

54
aw ɾe 'a na ðo 'sil
Aureana do sil
Golden girl of the Sil

as a 'ɾe naz de 'ow ɾu
As arenas de ouro,
The sands of gold

'son az ba 'ɣo as a 'se ðas
son as bagoas acedas
are the tears bitter

ke me 'fas tʃo 'ɾar 'ti
que me fas chorar ti.
that me you make cry you.

si 'ke ɾes 'ow ɾu 'fi nu
si queres ouro fino,
if you want gold fine,

'a βɾe u̯ 'mew ko ɾa 'son
abre o meu corazon:
open the my heart:

'tez de a to 'pa lo a 'li
tes de atopalo a li.
you have to find it there.

ko ke 'ko ʎas no 'ri o
Co que collas no rio,
With what you gather in the river,

As arenas de ouro,
aureana do Sil,
son asbagoas acedas
que me fas chorar ti.
Si queres ouro fino,
aureana do Sil,
abre o meu corazon
tés de a topalo a li.

Co que collas no rio,
aureana do Sil,
son asbagoas acedas
que me fas chorar ti.
Si queres ouro fino,
aureana do Sil,
abre o meu corazon
tés de a topalo a li.

————————●————————

The golden sands,
Aureana do Sil,
Are the bitter tears
That you make me cry.
If you want fine gold,
Aureana do Sil,
Open up my heart:
You will find it there.

mer ka 'ɾas 'kan du 'moj tu
mercaras   cando   moito
you will buy when   much

u na 'mo̯ ɾiŋ fe 'lis
un amor   infeliz.
a   love   unhappy.

'pa ɾa 'ðar kuŋ ka 'ɾi ɲu
para   dar c' un cariño
for   to find a loving

beɾða 'ðe ɾu 'az de   'βiɾ
verdadero   has de   vir
true   you must come

en ʃoj 'taɾ uz 'mewz 'o ʎos
enxoitar   os meus ollos,
bewitch   the my   eyes

aw ɾe 'a na ðo   'sil
Aureana   do   Sil.
Golden girl of the Sil.

With what you gather from the
river,
Aureana do Sil,
You will buy, at most,
An unhappy love.
If you want to find a true love,
You must come
To bewitch my eyes,
Aureana do Sil.

VI. *Dos canciones*

(*Two Songs*)

"Pastoral" (Pastoral)
"Llueve sobre el río" (Rain on the River)

Need we insist on the significance of pathways at dusk? These "Two Songs" follow poems by the famed Spanish poet Juan Ramón Jiménez (1881–1958), who won the Nobel prize in literature in 1956.

55
pas to 'ral
Pastoral
Pastoral

los ka 'mi noz ðe la 'tar ðe
Los caminos   de la tarde
The pathways   of the afternoon

se_____'a θen   'u no ˌkon la 'no tʃe
se   hacen   uno con la noche;
themselves they make one   with the night

por   'el 'e   ðe_'ir a 'ti
por   él he   de ir a ti,
through it I have to go to you

a 'mor ke   'tan to   t(e)_es 'kon des
amor   que tanto   te escondes.
love   that so much you you hide

Los caminos de la tarde
se hacen uno con la noche;
por él he de ir a ti,
amor que tanto te escondes.

Por él he de ir a ti
como la luz de los montes,
como la brisa del mar,
como el olor de las flores.

———————— • ————————

The pathways of noon
They all become one at night.
On that path I will come to you,
Love that hides so often.

On that path I will come to you
Like the light of the mountains,
Like the breeze of the sea,
Like the fragrance of the flowers.

poɾ   'el 'e   ðe‿'iɾ a 'ti
Por   él he   de ir a ti
Through it I have to go to you

'ko mo la 'luθ ðe loz 'mon tes
como   la luz de los montes,
like   the light of the mountains

'ko   mo la 'βɾi sa ðel 'mar
como la brisa del   mar,
like   the breeze of the sea

'ko mo‿el o 'lor   ðe las 'flo ɾes
como   el olor   de las flores.
like   the fragrance of the flowers

56
'ʎwe βe 'so βɾe‿(e)l 'ri o
Llueve sobre el río
It rains over the river

'ʎwe βe so βɾe‿(e)l 'ri o
Llueve sobre el río.
It rains over   the river

el   'a ɣwa‿es tɾe 'me θe
El agua   estremece
The water   makes shiver

los fɾa 'ɣan tes 'xuŋ kos
los fragantes juncos
the fragrant   bulrushes

de la‿o 'ɾi ʎa 'βer ðe
de la orilla   verde.
of the bank   green

Llueve sobre el río.
El agua estremece
los fragantes juncos
de la orilla verde.
¡Ay! qué ansioso olor
a pétalo frío.

Llueve sobre el río.
Mi barca parece mi sueño
en un vago mundo.
Orilla verde,
¡Ay!, barca sin junco.
¡Ay! Corazón frío.
Llueve sobre el río.

'aj 'ke‿an sjo so‿(o) loɾ
¡Ay! Qué ansioso olor
Oh What anxious smell

a 'pe ta lo 'fɾi o
a pétalo frío.
to petal cold

'ʎwe βe 'so βɾe (e)l 'ri o
Llueve sobre el río.
It rains over the river

mi 'βar ka pa 're θe mi 'swe ɲo
Mi barca parece mi sueño
My boat seems my dream

en um 'βa ɣo 'mun do
en un vago mundo.
in a vague world

o 'ri ʎa 'βer ðe
Orilla verde,
bank green

'aj 'βar ka siŋ 'xuŋ ko
¡Ay! barca sin junco.
Oh boat without bulrush

'aj ko ɾa 'θon 'fɾi o
¡Ay! Corazón frío.
Oh Heart cold

'ʎwe βe 'so βɾe (e)l 'ri o
Llueve sobre el río.
It rains over the river

It's raining on the river
The water makes
The fragrant rushes shiver
On the green bank.
Oh! What an anxious perfume
Of cold petals.

It's raining on the river.
My boat seems to be my dream
In a vague world.
Green bank,
Oh, boat without bulrushes.
Oh, cold heart.
It's raining on the river.

VII. *Becquerianas*

(*Bécquer Songs*)

"Hoy la tierra y los cielos me sonrien" (Today the Earth
and the Heavens Smile at Me)
"Los invisibles átomos del aire" (The Invisible Atoms of
the Air)
"Yo soy ardiente, yo soy morena" (I Am Fiery, I Am Dark)
"Yo se qual el objeto" (I Know the Reason)
"Volverán las oscuras golondrinas" (They Will Be Back,
the Dark Swallows)
"Olas Gigantes" (Gigantic Waves)

With the double title of *Cançons* and *Becquerianas*, Tenora
Edicions Musicals of Barcelona in 1980 published six songs of
Mompou. They are all based on poems by Gustavo Adolfo
Bécquer (1836–1870) from the posthumous collection of his
verse called *Rimas*. Bécquer, a late Romantic, is probably the
best known and the most popularly admired and read of all
Spanish poets, even today. His work is considered by his-
torians of Spanish literature as the most genuine of the
Romantic, ardent voices of Spain. Out of modesty, Bécquer
called his poems *Rimas*, literally 'Rhymes'; a closer rendering
in English would be 'verse'. Many of Bécquer's *Rimas* have
been memorized and recited by generations of Spaniards from
all walks of life. The choice of Bécquer's verse, although not
devoid of the puzzled and introspective vision of nature that
characterizes Mompou's other poetic choices, represents a
definite change in the composer's taste.

The songs correspond, in the order given them by
Mompou, to the following *Rimas* in Bécquer's standard
editions: 17, 10, 11, 59, 53, and 52. This last *rima* was also put
to music by Falla and is transcribed and translated on p. 118.
Here we simply reproduce the text.

57

'oj la 'tje ra j los 'θje los me son 'ri en
Hoy la tierra y los cielos me sonrien
Today the earth and the heavens me they
smile

'oj   la   'tje ra j   los 'θje los
Hoy la tierra y   los cielos
Today the earth and the heavens

me son 'ri en
me sonríen,
me they smile

'oj 'ʎe ɣa   (a)l   'fon do ðe
hoy llega   al   fondo de
today arrives to the bottom of

mj 'al ma el 'sol
mi alma el sol,
my soul   the sun

'oj   la 'e   'βis to la 'e   'βis to
hoy la he   visto… la he   visto
today her I have seen   her I have seen

j   me 'a   mi ɾa ðo
y   me ha   mirado,
and me she has looked at

'oj   kɾe o   en 'djos
¡hoy creo   en Dios!
today I believe in God

Hoy la tierra y los cielos me
sonríen,
hoy llega al fondo de mi alma el
sol,
hoy la he visto…, la he visto y
me ha mirado,
¡hoy creo en Dios!
¡Hoy creo en Dios!
¡Hoy creo en Dios!
¡Hoy creo en Dios!¹²

————— • —————

Today the earth and the heavens
smile at me,
Today the sun reaches the bottom
of my soul,
Today I saw her…, I saw her,
and she looked at me.
Today I believe in God!

58
los im bi 'si ßles 'a to moz del 'aj ɾe
Los invisibles átomos del aire
The invisible atoms of the air

los im bi 'si ßles 'a to moz del   'aj ɾe
Los invisibles   átomos   del   aire
The invisible   atoms   of the air

en de re 'ðor pal 'pi tan i
en derreder palpitan   y
     around   they beat   and
se_____jɱ 'fla man
se   inflaman;
themselves they flare

el 'θje lo se   de 'sa θe (e)n 'ra joz
el cielo se   deshace en   rayos
the sky   itself undoes   in   rays
de 'o ɾo
de oro;
of gold

la   'tje ra s(e) es tɾe 'me θe
la tierra se   estremece
the earth   itself shivers
al ßo ɾo 'θa ða
alborozada.
excited

'oj ɣo flo 'tan do en 'o laz de aɾ mo 'ni a
Oigo flotando   en olas   de armonía
I hear floating   in waves of harmony

Los invisibles átomos del aire
en derredor palpitan y se inflaman;
el cielo se deshace en rayos de oro;
la tierra se estremece alborozada.

Oigo flotando en olas de armonía
rumor de besos y batir de alas;
mis párpados se cierran...
¿qué sucede? ¿qué sucede?[13]
—Es el amor que pasa.
Es el amor que pasa.[14]

———————— • ————————

The invisible atoms of the air,
Around me, beat and flare;
The sky breaks out in golden rays;
The earth shivers in excitement.

I hear, as if floating in waves of harmony,
The rumor of kisses and the fluttering of wings;
My eyelids close..., what is happening, what is happening?
"It is love that went by.
It is love that went by."

ru 'mor ðe 'βe sos i   βa 'tir ðe‿'a las
rumor de besos y   batir de alas;
rumor of kisses and beating of wings

mis 'par pa ðos se 'θje ran
mis párpados se cierran...
my eyelids   themselves close

'ke su 'θe ðe 'ke su 'θe ðe
¿qué sucede? ¿qué sucede?
what happens what happens

'es el a 'mor ke 'pa sa
—Es el amor que pasa.
It is the love   that passes

'es el a 'mor ke 'pa sa
—Es el amor que pasa.
It is the love   that passes

59
ˌɟo 'soj aɾ 'ðjen te ˌɟo 'soj mo 'ɾe na
Yo soy ardiente, yo soy morena
I am fiery, I am brunette

ˌɟo 'soj aɾ 'ðjen te ˌɟo 'soj mo 'ɾe na
—Yo soy ardiente, yo soy morena,
I   am fiery   I   am brunette

ˌɟo 'soj el 'sim bo lo ðe la pa 'sjon
yo soy el símbolo de la pasión;
I am the symbol   of the passion

de 'an sja ðe 'ɣo θes mj‿'al ma̯ e̦s 'ta 'ʎe na
de ansia de goces mi alma está llena.
of desire of pleasure my soul   is   full

—Yo soy ardiente, yo soy morena,
yo soy el símbolo de la pasión;
de ansia de goces mi alma está llena.
¿A mí me buscas?—No es a ti, no.

a 'mi me 'βus kas   no̯ 'es a 'ti 'no
¿A mí me buscas? — No es a ti, no.
me   you look for   Not is   to you   no.

mi 'fɾen t(e̯) es 'pa li ða mis 'tɾen θaz de 'o ɾo
—Mi frente es pálida; mis trenzas, de oro;
my forehead is pale   my tresses   of gold

'pwe ðo βɾin 'dar te 'ði tʃas   siŋ   'fin
puedo brindarte dichas sin fin;
I can   offer you   happiness without end

'ʝo ðe ter 'nu ɾa   'ɣwar ðo̯ un te 'so ɾo
yo de ternura guardo un tesoro.
I   of tenderness I keep   a   treasure

a   'mi me 'ʎa mas 'no   no̯ 'es a 'ti
¿A mí me llamas? —No; no es a ti.
To me   you call No   not it is to you

ˌʝo 'soj   un 'swe ɲo un im po 'si βle
—Yo soy un sueño, un imposible,
I am   a   dream   an impossibility

'ba no fan 'taz ma ðe 'nje βla̯ j   'luθ
vano fantasma de niebla y luz;
vain   ghost   of fog   and light

'soj in kor 'po ɾe̯ a 'soj in taŋ 'xi βle
soy incorpórea, soy intangible;
I am incorporeal   I am intangible

no 'pwe ðo̯ a 'mar te̯ o   'βen 'ben 'tu
no puedo amarte. —¡Oh, ven; ven tú!
not I can   love you Oh   come come you

—Mi frente es pálida; mis trenzas, de oro;
puedo brindarte dichas sin fin;
yo de ternura[15] guardo un tesoro.
¿A mí me llamas?—No; no es a ti.

—Yo soy un sueño, un imposible,
vano fantasma de niebla y luz;
soy incorpórea, soy intangible;
no puedo amarte.—¡Oh, ven; ven tú!

———————•———————

I am fiery, I am dark,
I am the symbol of passion;
My soul is filled with a thirst for pleasure.
Is it I you are seeking?—No, it is not you.

My forehead is pale, my tresses are golden;
I can offer you boundless joy;
I hold a treasure of tenderness.
Is it I you are calling?—No, it is not you.

I am a dream, an impossibility,
An empty ghost made of mist and light;
I have no body, no one can touch me;
I cannot love you.—Oh come! Come!

60
'ɟo 'se 'kwal el oβ 'xe to
Yo se cual el objeto
I know which one the object

'ɟo 'se 'kwal el oβ 'xe to
Yo sé cuál el objeto
I know which one the object

de tus sus 'pi ɾos 'es
de tus suspiros es;
of your sighs it is

ko 'noθ ko 'ɟo la 'kaw sa ðe tu 'ðul θe
conozco yo la causa de tu dulce,
I know I the cause of your sweet

se 'kɾe ta lan gi 'ðeθ
secreta languidez.
secret languor

'te 'ri es al 'ɣun 'di a
¿Te ríes…? Algún día
You laugh? Some day

'sa 'βɾas 'ni ɲa por 'ke
sabrás, niña, por qué:
you'll know girl why

'tu a 'ka so lo sos 'pe tʃas
tú acaso lo sospechas
you perhaps it suspect

i 'ɟo lo 'se
y yo lo sé.
and I it know

Yo sé cuál el objeto
de tus suspiros es;
conozco yo[16] la causa de tu dulce,
secreta languidez.
¿Te ríes…? Algún día
sabrás, niña, por qué:
tú acaso lo sospechas,
y yo lo sé.

Yo sé lo que tú sueñas,[17]
y lo que en sueños ves;
como en un libro puedo lo que
callas
en tu frente leer.
¿Te ríes…? Algún día
sabrás, niña, por qué:
tú acaso lo sospechas,
y yo lo sé.

Yo sé por qué te sonríes[18]
y lloras a la vez;
penetro en los senos misteriosos
de tu alma de mujer.
¿Te ríes…? Algún día
sabrás, niña, por qué:
tú mientras sientes mucho[19] y nada
sabes,
yo, que no siento ya, todo lo sé.

———————— • ————————

'ɟo 'se   lo   ke   'tu   'swe ɲas
Yo sé   lo   que tú   sueñas,
I   know what   you dream

i   lo   ke   (e)n 'swe ɲoz 'bes
y   lo   que en   sueños   ves;
and what   in   dreams   you see

'ko mo en un 'li βɾo 'pwe ðo lo   ke
como   en un libro puedo   lo   que
as   in a   book I can   what
'ka ʎas
callas
you keep quiet

en tu   'fɾen te   'le: r
en tu   frente   leer.
on your forehead read

te   'ri es   al 'ɣun 'di a
¿Te ríes ...?   Algún día
    You laugh? Some day

sa 'βɾas   'ni ɲa por 'ke
sabrás,   niña, por qué:
you'll know girl   why

'tu a 'ka so lo sos 'pe tʃas
tú acaso   lo sospechas
you perhaps it suspect

i   'ɟo lo 'se
y   yo lo sé.
and I   it know

I know the reason
For your sighs;
I know the cause of your sweet,
Secret languor.
You laugh? Some day, girl,
You'll know why:
Now you may suspect it,
But I know.

I know what you dream,
And what you see in your dreams;
What you don't tell I can
Read in your forehead like a book.
You laugh? Some day, girl,
You'll know why:
Now you may suspect it,
But I know.

I know why you smile
And weep at the same time;
I can fathom the mysteries
Of your woman's soul.
You laugh? Some day, girl,
You'll know why:
While you feel many things, and
know none,
I, who can no longer feel, know
all.

'ɟo 'se   por 'ke te son 'ri es
Yo sé   por qué te sonríes
I   know why   you smile

i   'ʎo ɾas a la 'βeθ
y   lloras a la vez;
and weep   at the time

pe 'ne tɾo͜ en los 'se noz mis te 'ɾjo sos
penetro   en los senos   misteriosos
I penetrate in the cavities mysterious

de tw͜ 'al ma   ðe mu 'xer
de tu   alma de mujer.
of your soul of woman

te 'ri es   al 'ɣun 'di a
¿Te ríes...?   Algún día
     you laugh? Some day

sa 'βɾas   'ni ɲa por 'ke
sabrás,   niña, por qué:
you'll know girl   why

'tu 'mjen tɾas 'sjen tes 'mu tʃo͜ j
tú   mientras sientes mucho y
you while   you feel much   and
'na ða 'sa βes
nada   sabes,
nothing you know

'ɟo ke no 'sjen to 'ɟa   'to ðo lo 'se
yo, que no siento ya,   todo lo sé.
I   who not I feel   anymore all   I know

61
bol ße 'ɾan las os 'ku ɾaz go lon 'dɾi nas
Volverán las oscuras golondrinas
They shall return the dark swallows

bol ße 'ɾan   las os 'ku ɾaz
Volverán   **las oscuras**
They shall return the dark
go lon 'dɾi nas
golondrinas
swallows

en tu   ßal 'kon sus   'ni ðos a kol 'ɣaɾ
en tu   **balcón sus**   **nidos a colgar,**
on your balcony   their nests   to hang

j 'o tɾa   'ßeθ kon el 'a la (a) sus
y   otra   vez con el ala   a   sus
and another time with the wing to its
kɾis 'ta les
cristales
glass panes

xu 'ɣan do ʎa ma 'ɾan
jugando   llamarán.
playing   they will call

pe ɾo̯ a 'ke ʎas ke̯ (e)l 'ßwe lo
Pero aquellas que el   vuelo
but   those   that the flight
re fɾe 'na ßan
refrenaban
refrained

Volverán las oscuras golondrinas
en tu balcón sus nidos a colgar,
y otra vez con el ala a sus cristales
jugando llamarán.

Pero aquellas que el vuelo refrenaban
tu hermosura y mi dicha al contemplar;
aquellas que aprendieron nuestros nombres,
ésas ..., ¡no volverán!

Volverán las tupidas madreselvas
de tu jardín las tapias a escalar,
y otra vez a la tarde, aún más hermosas,
sus flores se abrirán.

Pero aquellas cuajadas de rocío
cuyas gotas mirábamos temblar
y caer como lágrimas del día ...
ésas ..., ¡no volverán!

Volverán del amor en tus oídos
las palabras ardientes a sonar;
tu corazón, de su profundo sueño
tal vez despertará.

Pero mudo y absorto y de rodillas
como se adora a Dios ante su altar,
como yo te he querido ...,
desengáñate,
¡así ... no te querrán!

'ko mo se͜ a 'ðo ɾa (a) 'ðjos an te sw͜ al 'tar
como se adora a Dios ante su altar,
as   one adores   God before his altar

'ko mo 'ʝo t(e) 'e   ke 'ɾi ðo
como yo te he   querido…,
as   I you have loved
ðe seŋ 'ga ɲa te
desengáñate,
un-deceive yourself

a 'si ˌno te   ke 'ran
¡así… no te   querrán!
thus   not you they will love

62
Olas Gigantes

Olas gigantes que os rompéis bramando
en las playas desiertas y remotas,
envuelto entre las sábanas de espuma,
¡llevadme con vosotras!

Ráfagas de huracán, que arrebatáis
del alto bosque las marchitas hojas,
arrastrando en el ciego torbellino,
¡llevadme con vosotras!

Nubes de tempestad que rompe el rayo
y en fuego ornáis las desprendidas orlas,
arrebatado entre la niebla oscura,
¡llevadme con vosotras!

Llevadme, por piedad, adonde el vértigo
con la razón me arranque la memoria.
Por piedad!… Tengo miedo de quedarme
con mi dolor a solas!

*See page 118 for IPA and translation.

VIII. *Three Songs*

"Primeros pasos" (First Steps)
"Fes-me la vida transparent" (Make My Life Transparent)
"Cantar del alma" (Song of the Soul)

This section gathers three fairly recent songs that were published independently. Two of them are based on modern poems of the Symbolist style. The first one, by Clara Janés—*Primeros pasos*, "First Steps"—is reminiscent of one of the Valéry poems. The second is by her father, the poet of the *Combat del somni* cycle: *Fesme la vida transparent*, "Make my life transparent".

The third song follows the well-known poem by Saint John of the Cross. It is an evocative, mystical work. The refrain *Aunque es de noche*, "Even though it is night", runs through the poem like a stream—and a stream from a fountain is indeed the other recurring metaphor of the piece. The night symbolizes at once negative, human oblivion and the possibility of the mystical experience. Only by reaching down to the black bottom of night may one awake to new life. The poem, using a very simple, repetitive pattern, is reminiscent of popular poetry. Its theme is the Eucharist but, clothed in images that may have antithetical mesnings—night, cold water—, the poem goes beyond mere devoutness. The final effect is a magical feeling that was surely what attracted Mompou to it.

63
pɾi 'me ɾos 'pa sos
Primeros pasos
First steps

tu   'kwer po 'ko mo̦ u̦n 'ar βol
Tu   cuerpo   como   un árbol,
Your body   like   a   tree

tus   'o xos   'ko mo̞ un   'la ɣo
tus   ojos   como   un lago,
your eyes   like   a   lake

i   'ɟo so 'ɲa βa̞ u̞n 'dir me
y   yo soñaba   hundirme
and I   dreamed   to drown myself

de 'βa xo   ðe tu̞   a 'βra θo
debajo   de tu   abrazo.
underneath of   your embrace

tu   'tjeŋ po no̞ 'e ɾa   tjeŋ po
Tu   tiempo   no era   tiempo,
Your time   not it was time

tu   'seɾ   'e ɾa u̞m mi 'la ɣɾo
tu   ser   era un milagro
your being was a   miracle

i   te   βus 'ke̞   'as ta (a) 'ʎar te
y   te   busqué   hasta hallarte
and you I searched for until   finding you

de 'βa xo   ðe tu̞   a 'βra θo
debajo   de tu   abrazo.
underneath of   your embrace

el   'sol mu 'ɾjo̞ en el   θje lo
El   sol   murió en el   cielo,
The sun died   in the sky

tus   'pa sos se̞ a le 'xa ɾon
tus   pasos   se alejaron
your steps   went far away

Tu cuerpo como un árbol,
tus ojos como un lago,
y yo soñaba hundirme
debajo de tu abrazo.
Tu tiempo no era tiempo,
tu ser era un milagro
y te busqué hasta hallarte
debajo de tu abrazo.
El sol murió en el cielo,
tus pasos se alejaron
y se quedó mi sueño
debajo de tu abrazo.

Your body like a tree,
Your eyes like a lake,
And I dreamed I was sinking
Under your embrace.
Your time was not time,
Your being was a miracle
And I sought you until I found
you
Under your embrace.
The sun died in the sky,
Your steps went away
And my dream was left
Under your embrace.

i   se ke 'ðo   mi 'swe ɲo
y   se quedó   mi sueño
and   remained my dream

de 'βa xo   ðe tu͜   a 'βra θo
debajo   de tu   abrazo.
underneath of your embrace

64
'fez mə lə 'βi ðə trəns pə 'ɾen
Fes-me la vida transparent
Make me the life transparent

'fez mə   lə   'βi ðə trəns pə 'ɾen
Fes-me   la   vida   transparent,
Make me the life   transparent

'kom əɫs 'tewz 'uʎs
com els teus ulls;
like   the your eyes

tor nə 'βen 'pu ɾə lə   'ma   'me βə
torna ben pura la mà   meva,
turn   very pure   the hand mine

j͜ əɫ   pən sə 'men
i   al   pensament
and to the thought

'du mi   lə 'paw
duu- m' hi   la pau.
bring me there the peace

Fes-me la vida transparent,
com els teus ulls;
torna ben pura la mà meva,[20]
i al pensament
duu-m'hi la pau.
Altra aventura no vull,
sinó la de seguir
l'estela blanca que neixia
dels teus camins.
I no llanguir
per ser mirall d'uns ulls.
Voldria ser com un riu oblidadís
que es lliura al mar,
les aigües pures de tota imatge
amb un anhel de blau.
I ser llavors feliç
de viure lluny d'amors obscures
amb l'esperança del teu cel.

'əɫ trə (ə) βen 'tu ɾa 'no 'βuʎ
Altra aventura   no vull,
Other adventure   not I want

si 'no lə də sə 'ɣi
sinó la de seguir
but   the of following

ləs 'tɛ lə 'βlaŋ kə kə nə 'ʃi ə   ðəɫs
l'estela blanca que neixia   dels
the wake white   that was born from the
'tews kə 'mins
teus camins.
your pathways

i   'no ʎən 'ɣi   pər 'se   mi 'ɾaʎ
I   no llanguir per ser   mirall
And not to languish for to be mirror
dunz uʎs
d'uns ulls.
of   eyes

bul 'ðɾi ə   'se   'kom un 'riw u βli ðə 'dis
Voldria   ser   com un riu   oblidadís
I would like to be like   a   river forgetful

kə (ə)z 'ʎiw ɾə (ə)ɫ   'mar
que es lliura   al   mar,
that itself abandons to the sea

ləz 'aj ɣwəs 'pu ɾəz ðə 'to tạ i 'ma dʒə
les aigües pures de tota   imatge
the waters   pure of all   image

əm un ə 'nɛɫ   ðə 'βlaw
amb un anhel   de blau.
with a   yearning for blue

Make my life transparent,
Like your eyes;
Make my hand pure,
And bring peace
To my thoughts.
I want no other adventure
Than to follow
The white wake left
By your passage.
And not to languish
For being the mirror of your eyes.
I would like to be a forgetful river
Giving itself to the sea,
The pure waters of all images
Craving for the blue.
And to be happy then
Living away from dark loves
With hope for your heaven.

i   'se   ʎə 'βɔs fə 'lis
I   ser   llavors feliç
And to be then   happy

də 'βiw ɾə 'ʎuɲ də 'morz ups 'ku ɾəs
de viure   lluny d' amors obscures
of living   far from loves   dark

əm   ləs pə 'ɾan sə ðəl   'tew 'sɛɫ
amb l' esperança del   teu cel.
with the hope   of the your heaven

65
kan 'tar ðel 'al ma
Cantar del alma
Song of the soul

A 'ke ʎa e 'ter na 'fwen te (e)s 'ta
Aquella eterna   fuente está
That   eternal   fountain is
es kon 'di ða
escondida,
hidden

ke   'βjen 'se   'ɟo 'ðo   tje ne su
que bien sé   yo dó   tiene su
That well know I   where it has its
ma 'ni ða
manida,
place

ˌawŋ k(e)   'ez de no tʃe
aunque   es de noche.
Even though it is by night

Aquella eterna fuente está
escondida,
que bien sé yo dó tiene su manida,
Aunque es de noche.
Su origen no lo sé, pues no le
tiene,
mas sé que todo origen de ella
viene,
aunque es de noche.
Sé que no puede ser cosa tan bella
y que cielos y tierra beben de ella,
aunque es de noche.
Aquesta [eterna] fuente está
escondida
en este vivo pan por darnos vida.
En esta noche oscura
que bien sé yo por fe la fontefrida.

su͜ o 'ri xen no lo 'se   ,pwes no le
Su origen no lo sé,   pues no le
Its origin   not it I know since not it
'tje ne
tiene,
has

ma(s) 'se   ke 'to ðo͜ (o) 'ri xen d(e) 'e ʎa
mas sé   que todo origen   de ella
But I know that every origin   from it
'βje ne
viene.
it comes

,awŋ k(e)   'ez de no tʃe
aunque   es de noche.
Even though it is by night

'se   ke no 'pwe ðe 'ser ko sa tam
Sé   que no puede ser cosa tan
I know that not it can be thing so
'be ʎa
bella
beautiful

i   ke 'θje los i   'tje ra 'βe βen
y   que cielos y   tierra beben
And that heavens and earth drink
d(e) 'e ʎa
de   ella,
from it

,awŋ k(e)   'ez de no tʃe
aunque   es de noche.
Even though it is by night

Sé ser tan caudalosas sus corrientes,
que infiernos, cielos riegan y las gentes,
aunque es de noche.
El corriente que nace de esta fuente
bien sé yo que es tan capaz y tan potente,
aunque es de noche.
Aquesta viva fuente que deseo
en este pan de vida yo la veo
aunque es de noche.

Aquella [eterna] fuente está escondida
que bien sé yo dó tiene su manida.
Su origen no lo sé, [pues no le tiene,]
Mas sé que todo origen de ella viene.[11]

a 'kes ta 'fwen te (e)s 'ta es kon 'di ða
Aquesta fuente   está   escondida
This   fountain is   hidden

en 'es te 'βi βo 'pan por 'ðar noz 'bi ða
en este   vivo pan   por darnos   vida.
In this   living bread to give us   life

en 'es ta 'no tʃe os 'ku ɾa
En esta   noche oscura,
On this   night dark

ke 'βjen 'se   ʝo por 'fe   la
que bien sé   yo por fe   la
That well I know I   by faith the
ˌfon te 'fri ða
fontefrida.
fountain cold

'se   'ser tan kaw ða 'lo sas sus
Sé   ser   tan caudalosas   sus
I know to be so abundant   its
ko 'rjen tes
corrientes,
streams

ke   im 'fjer nos 'θje los 'rje ɣan   i
que infiernos, cielos   riegan   y
That hells   heavens they water and
las 'xen tes
las gentes,
the people

ˌawŋ k(e)   'ez de no tʃe
aunque   es de noche.
Even though it is by night

That eternal fountain is hidden;
I know well where it lies,
Even though it is night.
I do not know its origin, since it has none,
But I know that every origin comes from it,
Even though it is night.
I know there cannot be anything as beautiful
And that heavens and earth drink from it,
Even though it is night.
This [eternal] fountain is hidden
In this living bread to give us life.
In this dark night.
For I know by faith it's the cold fountain,
I know its streams to be so full
That they water Hell, Heaven, and people,
Even though it is night.
The stream that pours forth from this fountain—
I know how capable it is, and how strong,
Even though it is night.
This living fountain that I desire—
I see it in this bread of life
Even though it is night.
That [eternal] fountain is hidden;
I know well where it lies.
I do not know its origin, [since it has none,]
But I know that every origin comes from it.

el   ko 'rjen te ke   'na θe ð(e) 'es ta
El   corriente   que nace   de   esta
The current   that is born from this
'fwen te
fuente
fountain

'bjen 'se   'ɟo k(e) 'es tan ka 'paθ
bien sé   yo que es   tan capaz
Well know I   that it is so capable
i   tam po 'ten te
y   tan potente,
and so   potent

ˌawŋ k(e)   'ez de no tʃe
aunque   es   de noche.
Even though it is by night

a 'kes ta 'βi βa 'fwen te ke   ðe 'se o
Aquesta viva   fuente   que deseo
This   living fountain that I desire

en 'es te 'pan de 'βi ða 'ɟo la 'βe o
en este   pan   de vida   yo la veo
In this   bread of life   I   it see

ˌawŋ k(e)   'ez de no tʃe
aunque   es   de noche.
Even though it is by night

a 'ke ʎa 'fwen te (e)s 'ta e̜s kon 'di ða
Aquella fuente   está   escondida
That   fountain is   hidden

ke 'βjen 'se   'ɟo 'ðo   'tje ne su ma 'ni ða
que bien sé   yo dó   tiene su manida.
That well know I   where it has its place.

su‿o 'ri xen 'no lo 'se
Su origen   no lo sé,
Its origin   not it I know

ma(s) 'se   ke   'to ð(o)‿o 'ri xen d(e)‿'e ʎa
mas sé   que todo   origen de   ella
But   I know that every   origin   from it
'βje ne
viene.
it comes

IX. *French Songs*: *Le Nuage* and *Charmes*

"Le Nuage" (The Cloud)
"La fausse morte" (The False Dead)
"L'insinuant" (The Hinter)
"Le Sylphe" (The Sylph)
"Le vin perdu" (Lost Wine)
"Les pas" (The Steps)

Our final section gathers the songs Mompou wrote based on French poems. The first song is by Mathilde Pomès, who must have been an acquaintance of the composer from his many years in France. The rest are based on poems from the book *Charmes* by Valéry. A note on these precedes the translations. We are including these French songs merely to make the volume complete. Our purpose is to provide a panorama of Spanish songs of the twentieth century, and thus we limit ourselves to rendering the text with a translation.

66
Le Nuage
The cloud

S'embarquer, ô lente nef,
à ton bord sans capitaine;
s'embarquer, ô blanc vaisseau,
à ton bord sans gouvernail,
rompues les amarres du souvenir même,
perdu le sextant du désir concret.
Aller voguer dans une douce dérive,
sur une mer sans couleur
vers des îles sans contour.
Voguer, aller, aller...
Le silence diaphane
tenant lieu pour espace,
le coeur ne martelant plus
la scansion des secondes
qu'en battements étouffés.
Aller voguer, voguer
a chaque coup de roulis
perdre un peu de sa figure,
perdre un peu de sa substance.
Voguer, aller
jusqu'à ce point idéal
où la mer du ciel se comble
pour baigner le clair visage
d'une terre plus fleurie;
mon esquif plus frêle
que neige en avril,
fondue au soleil la haute misaine,
l'étrave rongée par les alizés,
du beau port en vue
mollement couler...

————— ● —————

To embark, oh slow ship,
On your board that has no captain;
To embark, oh white vessel,
On your board that has no helmsman,
The mooring ropes of memory itself broken,
The sextant of concrete desire lost.
To go sailing in a sweet drift,
On a colorless sea
With shapeless islands.
To sail, to go, to go ...
The diaphanous silence
With place in space,
The heart now hammering
The scansion of seconds
With a stifled beat.
To go sailing, sailing
With every roll
Losing a bit of one's form,
Losing a bit of one's substance.
To sail, to go
To that ideal point
Where the sea fills with sky
To bathe the bright face
Of a more flowered land;
My skiff more frail
Than snow in April,
The high foresail melted in the sun,
The stem post gnawed at by trade winds,
Within sight of the beautiful port
Gently gliding ...

A note on *Charmes*

We have given the title *Charmes* to this series of five songs for voice and piano that Mompou wrote for five poems by Paul Valéry from his book of the same title. The word *charmes* means, of course 'charms'; it is related, other than to grace and enchantment, to the Latin word *carmen*, 'song', which appears in the frontispiece of Valéry's collection: *Deducere carmen*, 'To bring down the song'. *Charmes* is Valery's best-known collection of poems; it includes his famed "Le Cimetière marin". But Mompou has chosen five shorter pieces from *Charmes* and rearranged them in the order given here.

Mompou is interested in suggestive poetry, and he is at home in this post-impressionistic period of Valéry's. A neo-romantic suggestiveness is the predominant tone in these songs, mainly in songs I and V. "The False Dead" relates the paradox of a lover who, upon fainting on his beloved's tomb, is revived by the falsely dead image on the stone. "The Steps" unites the quiet noise of the beloved's tread with the beating of the lover's heart. In between these two love poems are three more playful pieces: "The Sylph" is a period piece almost palpable in its art-deco Greek revivalism. In "Lost Wine" we have a ceremonious transition to the more serious love theme that encloses the series.

Valéry's poems are mostly made up of long, inconclusive sentences; in their French original the poems are constantly playing with sounds and repetition of sounds. The whole poetic enterprise seems to suggest a mystery-laden, overheard, incomplete expression reverberating in the still air of timelessness.

67
La fausse morte
The false dead

Humblement, tendrement, sur le tombeau charmant,
Sur l'insensible monument,
Que d'ombres, d'abandons, et d'amour prodiguée,
Forme ta grâce fatiguée,
Je meurs, je meurs sur toi, je tombe et je m'abats,
Mais à peine abattu sur le sépulcre bas,
Dont la close étendue aux cendres me convie,
Cette morte apparente, en qui revient la vie,
Frémit, rouvre les yeux, m'illumine et me mord,
Et m'arrache toujours une nouvelle mort
Plus précieuse que la vie.

———— • ————

Humbly, tenderly, upon the enchanting tomb,
Over the insensitive monument
That, prodigal with shadows, abandon, and love,
Forms your exhausted grace,
I die, I die over you. I fall and subside,
But having now collapsed on the low sepulchre
Whose stone, spread over the ashes, invites me,
This feigned dead, in whom life returns,
Quivers, opens her eyes again, illuminates and bites me,
And tears me out, always to a new death,
More precious than life.

68
L'insinuant
The hinter

O courbes, méandre,
Secrets du menteur,
Est-il art plus tendre
Que cette lenteur?

Je sais où je vais,
Je t'y veux conduire,
Mon dessein mauvais
N'est pas de te nuire…

(Quoique souriante
En pleine fierté,
Tant de liberté
La désoriente!)

O courbes, méandre,
Secrets du menteur,
Je veux faire attendre
Le mot le plus tendre.

————— • —————

Oh curves, oh meanders,
Secrets of the liar.
Is there an art more tender
Than this slow pace?

I know where I go,
There I will take you;
My evil design
Is not to harm you.

(Although she smiles
With a fierce expression,
So much freedom
Disorients her!)

Oh curves, oh meanders,
Secrets of the liar,
I will make her wait
For that most tender word.

69
Le sylphe
The sylph

Ni vu ni connu
Je suis le parfum
Vivant et défunt
Dans le vent venu!

Ni vu ni connu,
Hasard ou génie?
A peine venu
La tâche est finie!

Ni lu ni compris?
Aux meilleurs esprits
Que d'erreurs promises!

Ni vu ni connu
Le temps d'un sein nu
Entre deux chemises!

———— • ————

Neither seen nor known,
I am the perfume,
Living and dead,
That came with the wind!

Neither seen nor known,
Am I Fate or Genius?
Having just come
My task is done!

Neither read nor understood?
To the finest of spirits
How many promised errors!

Neither seen nor known,
The moment for a naked breast
In between two shirts!

70
Le vin perdu
Lost wine

J'ai, quelque jour, dans l'océan,
(Mais je ne sais plus sous quels cieux),
Jeté, comme offrande au néant,
Tout un peu de vin précieux...

Qui voulut ta perte, ô liqueur?
J'obéis, peut-être au devin?
Peut-être au souci de mon coeur,
Songeant au sang, versant le vin?

Sa transparence accoutumée
Après une rose fumée
Reprit aussi pure la mer...

Perdu ce vin, ivres les ondes!...
J'ai vu bondir dans l'air amer
Les figures les plus profondes...

———————— • ————————

One day, in the ocean
(But I no longer know under what skies)
I threw, as an offering to nothingness,
A little bit of precious wine...

Who willed this wasting, oh liquor?
Did I perchance obey the soothsayer?
Or perchance the restlessness of my heart,
Dreaming of blood, spilling the wine?

Its usual transparence,
After becoming a pink cloudspread,
Was taken so purely by the sea...

Lost the wine, drunken the waves!...
I saw bouncing in the bitter air
The most profound figurations...

71
Les pas
The steps

Tes pas, enfants de mon silence,
Saintement, lentement placés,
Vers le lit de ma vigilance
Procèdent muets et glacés.

Personne pure, ombre divine,
Qu'ils sont doux, tes pas retenus!
Dieux!... tous les dons que je devine
Viennent à moi sur ces pieds nus!

Si, de tes lèvres avancées,
Tu prépares, pour l'apaiser
A l'habitant de mes pensées
La nourriture d'un baiser,

Ne hâte pas cet acte tendre,
Douceur d'être et de n'être pas,
Car j'ai vécu de vous attendre,
Et mon coeur n'était que vos pas.

Your steps, children of my silence,
Saintly, slowly placed
Towards the bed of my vigil,
Advance quiet and frozen.

Pure person, divine shadow,
How sweet they are, your constrained steps!
Gods! ... All the gifts that I foresee
Come to me on those naked feet!

If, with your pursed lips,
You prepare, in order to appease
The inhabitant of my thoughts,
The nourishment of a kiss,

Do not halt this tender act,
Sweetness of being and being not,
For I lived waiting for you
And my heart, it was but your steps.

Biographies

Enrique Granados

1867–	Born in Lleida (Lérida), Catalonia, Spain.
1880's–	Begins piano studies in Barcelona.
1883–	Studies composition with Pedrell in Barcelona.
1887–89–	Studies with Charles Bériot in Paris. Meets Ricard Viñes.
1889–	Returns to Barcelona.
1892–	*Tres danzas españolas.*
1895–	Quintet for piano.
1898–	*María del Carmen* premieres in Madrid.
1899–	Founds the *Societat de concerts.*
1901–	Founds the *Academia Granados.*
1905–	Works with Casals, Thibaut, Malats, Saint-Saëns.
1908–	*Divina comedia.*
1911–	*Goyescas* piano suite premieres in Barcelona.
1912–	*Elisenda.*
1913–	*Goyescas* piano suite premieres in Madrid.
1914–	*Goyescas* piano suite premieres in Paris.
1916–	The opera *Goyescas* premieres at the Metropolitan, New York, January 28.
1916–	*Colección de tonadillas.*
1916–	Dies at sea.

Manuel de Falla

1876–	Born in Cadiz on November 23.
1896–1907–	Lives in Madrid. Meets Pedrell.
1899–1901–	Composes "Preludios," "Olas gigantes," "Dios mío…"
1904–05–	Composes *La vida breve* (opera), for which he is awarded a prize.
1907–14–	Lives in Paris.
1911–15–	*Noches en los jardines de España* (for piano and orchestra).
1913–	*La vida breve* premieres in Nice.
1914–	Returns to Madrid.
1914–	*La vida breve* premieres in Madrid's Teatro de la Zarzuela in November.
1914–	*Trois chansons.*
1914–15–	*Siete canciones populares españolas.*
	El amor brujo (ballet).
1914–16–	"El pan de Ronda."
1915–	"Oración de las madres…"
1916–	*Noël des enfants.*
1918–19–	Diaghilev commissions *El sombrero de tres picos* (ballet).
1919–	*Fantasía bética* (for piano).
1919–22–	*El retablo de maese Pedro* (opera).
1920–39–	Lives in Granada.
1922–	*Siete canciones populares españolas* published in Paris.
1923–	Concerto for Keyboard and Five Instruments.
1924–	*Psyché.*
1926–	Harpsichord concerto.
1934–	Succeeds Elgar in the Académie des Beaux Arts.
1939–	Exiled to Argentina.
1946–	Dies in Alta Gracia, Argentina, on November 14.
1980–	*Obras desconocidas.*

Frederic Mompou

1893–	Born in Barcelona on April 16.
1911–	Travels to Paris.
1913–	Returns to Barcelona.
1914–	*Impressions íntimes.*
1916–	"L'hora grisa."

195

1917–	"Escenes d'infants," "Pessebres," "Cants màgics."
1918–28–	*Cançons i danses.*
1920–	*Fêtes lointaines, Charmes.*
1921–	Returns to Paris.
1926–	"Cançoneta incerta." *Tres Comptines* 1–3.
1941–	Returns to Barcelona.
1948–	*Combat del somni.*
1949–	"Cançó de la fira."
1952–	Elected to the Acadèmia de Belles Arts.
1954–	*House of Birds.*
1955–	*Perlimplinada.*
1957–	"Cantar del alma."
1957–65–	*Música callada.*
1970–	*Improperiae. L'ocell daurat.*
1971–	*Becquerianas.*
1972–	*Cinc melodies.*
1973–	Named to the Academia de San Fernando (Madrid).
1976–	Receives the Gold Medal for Artistic Merit.
1977–	Prize, International Critics Club (Berlin). Doctor Honoris Causa, University of Barcelona.
1979–	Gold medal, Catalan government.

List of Published Songs

Song No.	Date of Composition	Title of Song	Composer	Poet
1		Amor y odio	Granados	Fernando Periquet
2		Callejeo	Granados	F. Periquet
3		El majo discreto	Granados	F. Periquet
4		El majo olvidado	Granados	F. Periquet
5		El mirar de la maja	Granados	F. Periquet
6		El majo tímido	Granados	F. Periquet
7		El tra-la-lá	Granados	F. Periquet
8		La maja de Goya	Granados	F. Periquet
9–11		La maja dolorosa	Granados	F. Periquet
12		Las currutacas	Granados	F. Periquet
13		Si al retiro	Granados	
14		Canto gitano	Granados	
15–21		*Canciones amatorias*	Granados	
22		Elegia eterna	Granados	Apel.les Mestres
23		L'ocell profeta	Granados	Countess of Castellar
24–30	1914–15	*Siete Canciones pop.*	Falla	Popular texts
31	1902	Tus ojillos negros	Falla	Cristóbal de Castro
32	1899	Preludios	Falla	Antonio de Trueba
33	1899	Olas gigantes	Falla	G. A. Bécquer
34	1899	Dios mío	Falla	G. A. Bécquer
35	1914	Oración	Falla	Martínez Sierra
36	1915	El pan de Ronda	Falla	Martínez Sierra
37–9	1926	*Tres comptines*	Mompou	Popular texts
40–2	1943	*Tres comptines*	Mompou	Popular texts
43	1942	Damunt de tu	Mompou	Josep Janés
44	1946	Aquesta nit	Mompou	Josep Janés
45	1948	Jo et pressentia	Mompou	Josep Janés
46–9	1925	*Quatre mélodies*	Mompou	Mompou
50	1949	Cançó de la fira	Mompou	Tomàs Garcés
51	1926	Cançoneta incerta	Mompou	Josep Carner
52	1916	L'hora grisa	Mompou	Manuel Blancafort
53	1962	Sant Martí	Mompou	Pere Ribot
54	1951	Aureana do Sil	Mompou	Ramón Cabanillas
55	1945	Pastoral	Mompou	Juan Ramón Jiménez
56	1945	Llueve sobre el río	Mompou	Juan Ramón Jiménez
57–62	1971	*Becquerianas*	Mompou	G. A. Bécquer
63	1964	Primeros pasos	Mompou	Clara Janés
64	1951	Fes-me la vida	Mompou	Josep Janés
65	1951	Cantar del alma	Mompou	St John of the Cross
66		Le nuage	Mompou	Mathilde Pomès
67–71	1920	*Charmes*	Mompou	Paul Valéry

Song No.	Date of Publication	Publisher	Dedication
1	1913	Unión Musical Española, Madrid	María Barrientos
2	1913	Unión Musical Española	María Barrientos
3	1913	Unión Musical Española	
4	1913	Unión Musical Española	Emilio de Gogorza
5	1913	Unión Musical Española	
6	1913	Unión Musical Española	
7	1913	Unión Musical Española	
8	1913	Unión Musical Española	
9–11	1913	Unión Musical Española	
12	1913	Unión Musical Española	

Song No.	Date of Publication	Publisher	Dedication
13	1971	Unión Musical Española	
14	1971	Unión Musical Española	
15–21	1962	Unión Musical Española	Concepció Badia
22	1962	Unión Musical Española	
23	1962	Unión Musical Española	
24–30	1922	M. Eshig, Paris	Mme. Ida Godebska
31	1940	Unión Musical Española	Sres. de Alta Villa
32	1980	Unión Musical Española	
33	1980	Unión Musical Española	
34	1980	Unión Musical Española	
35	1980	Unión Musical Española	
36	1980	Unión Musical Española	
37–9	1931	Rouart Lerolle & Co., Paris	Jane Bathori
40–2	1955	Editions Salabert, Paris	
43	1949	Editions Salabert	
44	1949	Editions Salabert	
45	1949	Editions Salabert	
46–9	1931	Rouart Lerolle	
50	1949	Editions Salabert	
51	1953	Unión Musical Española	María Barrientos
52	1954	Unión Musical Española	Helise Paris de Blancafort
53	1982	Edicions Tenora, Barcelona	Anna Ricci
54	1951	Editions Salabert	
55	1945	Editions Salabert	
56	1945	Editions Salabert	
57–62	1980	Edicions Tenora	
63	1967	Editions Salabert	
64	1951	Editions Salabert	
65	1961	Editions Salabert	
66	1931	Rouart Lerolle	
67–71	1925	Max Eschig	

Index of Song Titles

Index of First Lines

Notes

[1] Repetition of phrase not in original poem.
[2] Repetition of word not in original poem.
[3] Original has *veient-se.*
[4] Last line not in original poem.
[5] Original score has *sacorsa,* a nonexistent word.
[6] Line not in original poem.
[7] Repetition of phrase not in original poem.
[8] Repetition of line not in original poem.
[9] Poem continues with nine more stanzas.
[10] Original has *sabrà.*
[11] Repetition of line not in original poem.
[12] Repetition of line not in original poem.
[13] Repetition of phrase not in original poem.
[14] Repetition of phrase not in original poem.
[15] Original has *ternuras.*
[16] Original has *yo conozco.*
[17] Original has *Yo sé cuándo tú sueñas.*
[18] Original has *por qué sonríes.*
[19] Original has *mientras tú sientes mucho.*
[20] Original has *la meva mà.*
[21] This version represents a considerable rearrangement of the original poem. Compare the following traditional version:

> *Cantar de la alma que se huelga de concocer a Dios por fe*
>
> Que bien sé yo la fonte que mana y corre, aunque es de noche.
> Aquella eterna fonte está ascondida, que bien sé yo do tiene su manida, aunque es de noche.

Su origen no lo sé, pues no le tiene, mas sé que todo origen della viene, aunque es de noche.
Sé que no puede ser cosa tan bella, y que cielos y tierra beben de ella, aunque es de noche.
Bien sé que suelo en ella no se halla y que ninguno puede vadealla, aunque es de noche.
Su claridad nunca es escurecida, y sé que toda luz de ella es venida, aunque es de noche.
Sé ser tan caudalosos sus corrientes, que infiernos, cielos riegan, y las gentes, aunque es de noche.
El corriente que nace de esta fuente, bien sé que es tan capaz y omnipotente, aunque es de noche.
El corriente que de estas dos procede sé que ninguna de ellas le precede, aunque es de noche.
Aquesta eterna fonte está escondida en este vivo pan por darnos vida, aunque es de noche.
Aqui se está llamando a las criaturas, y de esta agua se hartan, aunque a escuras porque es de noche.
Aquesta viva fuente, que deseo, en este pan de vida yo la veo, aunque es de noche.

Reprinted from *Antología de la literatura española*, ed. Germän Bleiberg, Madrid: Alianza Editorial, 1969.